Famous Americans

22 Short Plays for the Classroom

SCHOLASTIC
PROFESSIONAL **B**OOKS

NEW YORK ▪ TORONTO ▪ LONDON ▪ AUCKLAND ▪ SYDNEY

The editor wishes to express appreciation to the many fine playwrights who contributed to this collection. Special thanks to Sarah Glasscock, Helen H. Moore, Timothy Nolan, Wendy Murray, Jackie Swensen, and Mona Mark for their dedication to this project.

Compiled and edited by Liza Schafer
Cover design by Vincent Ceci
Cover art by Claude Martinot
Interior design by Jacqueline Swensen
Interior illustration by Mona Mark

ISBN 0-590-49474-0

Contents

★★★★★★★★★★★★★

Introduction 5

Christopher Columbus: *Searching for the Indies* 9

Ben Franklin: *Philosopher, Inventor, Community Activist* 18

George Washington: *A Soldier, a Peaceful Man* 26

Phillis Wheatley: *Voice of Freedom* 35

Meriwether Lewis and William Clark: *Their Excellent Adventure* 45

Davy Crockett: *Hero of the Frontier* 52

Abraham Lincoln: *Holding the Nation Together* 60

Susan B. Anthony: *The Fight for Women's Rights* 67

Harriet Tubman: *Guide to Freedom* 74

John Muir: *The Father of National Parks* 82

Thomas Edison and Alexander Graham Bell: *A Meeting of Two Minds* 91

George Washington Carver: *The Scientist Who Saved the South* 98

Susan LaFlesche Picotte: *An Omaha Doctor Returns Home* 107

Nellie Bly: *Investigative Reporter* 116

Orville and Wilbur Wright: *First in the Air* 125

Franklin Delano Roosevelt: *The Man Who Never Gave Up* 134

Amelia Earhart: *Flying into the Unknown* 142

Langston Hughes: *Finding the Words* 151

Rosa Parks and Martin Luther King, Jr.: *The Montgomery Bus Boycott* 161

Jackie Robinson: *At Home in the Major Leagues* 170

Cesar Chavez: *¡Viva La Causa!* 177

Neil Armstrong: *To the Moon!* 186

Introduction

★ ★ ★ ★ ★ ★ ★ ★ ★ ★ ★ ★ ★ ★ ★ ★ ★ ★ ★ ★

The history of our country is really a story of people—some blessed with extraordinary bravery, others whose quiet voices spoke eloquent volumes; some who were guided by noble vision, others who, through sheer force of will, changed the course of the country. These are the people who make up America. Through plays we can bring these extraordinary men and women to life and get a sense of the people behind the accomplishments. By seeing people for people, a human connection is established, a link that spans eras and generations. Making this connection is the purpose of drama, and seeing it is the key to appreciating history.

We hope you and your students enjoy the 22 plays in this collection. We certainly enjoyed researching and writing about the inspiring Americans whose stories unfold on these pages.

OUR PURPOSE

The readers' theater plays in this book are intended to enrich classroom learning in a number of ways. They will:

☆ build oral literacy

☆ foster a knowledge of our American heritage

☆ encourage an appreciation of acting and the theater

☆ draw out quiet or at-risk students

☆ provide an exciting, hands-on, and student-centered format for learning.

Reading plays aloud is one of the most effective ways you can promote literacy and history in your classroom. We encourage you to invite students to perform these plays as a part of your social-studies or language-arts curriculum. (Before you begin, you might suggest readers spend a few moments "getting acquainted" with the characters they are playing by reading over their lines.)

USING THE PLAYS

HOW TO CAST

In writing these plays, every effort has been taken to make sure there are many different parts, as well as parts for both boys and girls. But don't be limited by what

is on the page. Students should be encouraged to read and play the parts of characters of different ethnicities and genders.

EXTENSION ACTIVITIES

At the end of every play you will find Extension Activities organized into Talk About It, Write About It, and Report About It sections. These activities are designed to focus the class on one or more of the themes of the play (dealing with racism in *Jackie Robinson: At Home in the Major Leagues,* perseverance and staying true to your vision in *First in the Air: The Story of the Wright Brothers,* etc.). The activities are meant to be used in conjunction with the plays, but by no means should you limit your discussion or lesson to what is presented. Rather, consider using these as a means to an end.

In the extension activities, you will find many opportunities for oral discussion and group work. Since one of the stated goals of presenting the plays is improving oral language skills, you may want to invite students to present reports to the class on one or more of the Americans profiled. These can be individual or group reports and may be presented to the class or to younger students during appropriate times of the year (Veteran's Day, Martin Luther King Day, Presidents' Day, Memorial Day, etc.). If you like, encourage the students to focus their reports on the themes of the plays, or a theme you and your class may have developed from your own classroom discussion.

Another way to build on the classroom activities is to encourage your students to write their own dramas. Again, they may do this individually or work in groups. For example, they could write their own play based on the life of the person they just read about; they could write about another chapter in the person's life; or they could write a play of fiction that is set in the same era. Try these suggestions or some others developed through your own classroom discussions.

Students may also enjoy a role-playing game. This works best when you are studying a period with many well-known and colorful characters (the signing of the Declaration of Independence or the drafting of the Constitution, for example). Write down the names of some or all of the major (and some minor) figures of the time, put the names in a hat, and have students draw the names. Invite students to research their roles, then bring everyone together to ad-lib the historic event. If you like, kids can also put together a report on the period based on what they have learned through the exercise. Such activities must be carefully moderated, but can really bring the study of the past into the present.

LARGER PERFORMANCES

You will find early on that students are very enthusiastic about reading plays. As ways of encouraging and nurturing their enthusiasm, think about other ways to perform the plays.

Since most of the plays have about ten characters, try assigning plays of the same historical era to groups in class and let them rehearse and perform the drama for the rest of the class. You could also organize a "play day" around an era or other theme (women in history, aviation, major figures of the twentieth century, etc.). Have the two or three groups perform the plays for the rest of the class, then initiate a discussion when all the plays are performed.

If you find that the class is enthusiastic and hungry for more performances, take the plays before the whole school—again, either organized around a holiday or a historical theme. Try calling on parents to get involved by donating or making costumes, building sets, making up posters and getting other publicity. You will find that many of these can be done cheaply and without much trouble—students can paint sets on large paper which can then be hung at the back of the stage; mom or grandma's old dress could become a period costume. This can be a great way to celebrate Women's History Month, Black History Month, or to observe Presidents' Day.

Christopher Columbus
Searching for the Indies

≈

by Frank Caropreso

Characters (in order of appearance):

NARRATOR
COLUMBUS: Leader and captain of the *Santa Maria*
QUEEN ISABELLA: Queen of Spain
KING FERDINAND: King of Spain
SPANISH SAILORS 1-3
RODRIGO DE TRIANA: First sailor to spot land
TAINO PEOPLE 1-3
RODRIGO SANCHEZ OF SEGOVIA: Secretary of the fleet
RODRIGO DE ESCOVEDA: The Queen's inspector
TRANSLATOR
TAINO CHIEF
TAINO MEN AND WOMAN 1-6 (nonspeaking roles)
MARTIN ALONZO PINZON: Captain of the *Pinta*
SPANISH SAILORS 1-3 (nonspeaking roles)

ACT 1

★★★★★★ SCENE: January 1492. Spain. Columbus enters the throne room where Ferdinand and Isabella are seated.

NARRATOR: For five long years, Christopher Columbus has been hoping that one of the monarchs of Europe would give him money to undertake a dangerous sea voyage. At last, the King and Queen of Spain agree to see him. Columbus's dream of reaching the East Indies by sailing west is in King Ferdinand and Queen Isabella's hands.

ISABELLA (impatiently): Approach. We know what you want, Columbus, but tell us—how would Spain benefit?

COLUMBUS (bowing deeply): My Queen, a faster route to the East Indies will give Spain control of the spice trade. It will bring you even greater glory, more gold, and more converts to Christianity.

ISABELLA (whispering to the King): We have so little to lose and so much to gain. If he's right, Spain will rule the world.

FERDINAND (doubtfully): I'm not so sure—

ISABELLA: Very well, Columbus. We will support you. You shall have all you need. In return, Spain claims all new lands you discover.

COLUMBUS (bowing deeply): Oh, yes, certainly, yes. And—for my small troubles, your majesties—all I ask for is ten percent of all the riches I bring back to you. And—as your servant—I ask to be made governor of the new territories.

FERDINAND (angrily): Now just a minute—

ISABELLA (pretending to be angry): You have very big dreams, Columbus. (smiling) But—we agree. Bring us back something interesting. Now, on your way.

COLUMBUS: Your majesties.

(He bows and walks backward to the door.)

ACT 2

★★★★★★ SCENE: October 10, 1492. Three sailors, Columbus, and Rodrigo de Triana are on the deck of the Santa Maria.

NARRATOR: And so, on August 3, 1492, Columbus sailed from Spain. He was given three ships: the *Niña*, the *Pinta*, and the *Santa Maria* and a crew of 100 men. After three months at sea, the crew was scared and wanted to turn back.

SAILOR 1: Our food and water are running out.

SAILOR 2: Columbus is nothing but a liar. We should have reached the Indies by now. We were never meant to go this far.

SAILOR 3: Let's kill him! We'll take over the ship and turn it around.

SAILOR 1: No let's keep sailing a while longer. It might rain.

COLUMBUS (overhearing the sailors): What's the trouble, men?

SAILOR 2 (with anger): This trip is cursed. There—I've said it. We want to go home.

COLUMBUS: Nonsense. We're right on course. We'll reach land soon. Very soon. Remember, we're doing this for Spain, and our gentle Queen.

SAILOR 3 (whispering to the other sailors): Gentle? He must be talking about another Queen Isabella. She burns her enemies at the stake! (louder) I'm here because of the gold!

SAILOR 2: Shh, idiot! Do you want him to hear you?

(The sailors slink back to their duties.)

NARRATOR: Columbus *is* worried, but three days later there's a sign that land is near.

RODRIGO DE TRIANA (scooping a branch with pink flowers from the sea): Look!

COLUMBUS: Yes! (giving Rodrigo de Triana a high five) What did I tell you? This branch was growing on a tree not more than three days ago.

(Everyone cheers.)

ACT 3
★ ★ ★ ★ ★ **SCENE 1: The coast of Guanahani. Three Taino people are fishing on the beach. Columbus and his party are about to land on the beach.**

NARRATOR: That branch probably came from Guanahani, an island about 400 miles south of Miami, Florida. It was the home of the Taino people. Guanahani was the first island on which Columbus and his men set foot. Unfortunately, Columbus believed he had reached an island off the coast of Japan or China.

TAINO 1 (shading eyes): What's that in the water?

TAINO 2: Looks like boats. Three of them. They're headed this way.

TAINO 3 (to Taino 1): Go tell the chief we've got company. We'll see what the strangers want.

(Taino 1 leaves.)

TAINO 2 (pointing): There they are, on the beach—past those trees. But what are they doing?

(Columbus kneels down and kisses the sand. Then he stands up and plants the flag of Queen Isabella and King Ferdinand on the beach.)

TAINO 3: The tall one is licking the sand. He must be very hungry.

(Filled with curiosity, they walk to Columbus and his men.)

COLUMBUS: I claim this land in the name of her majesty, Queen Isabella, and Spain. I name it San Salvador. Have you ever seen such a beautiful green island in all your days, Sanchez?

RODRIGO SANCHEZ: Never, Admiral. It shines like an emerald.

RODRIGO DE ESCOVEDO: We must be very close to the coast of China or Japan. The Queen will be pleased.

RODRIGO DE TRIANO (pointing to the Tainos approaching): Ho! Visitors!

NARRATOR: The Tainos approached the landing party. They didn't speak Spanish, and the Spaniards didn't speak the Taino language. With much hand waving and smiling, the groups succeeded in communicating with each other. We'll pretend that we can understand everything everyone is saying.

TAINO 2 (to Columbus): Welcome to our home.

COLUMBUS (smiling and speaking to the translator): Did you understand any of that?

TRANSLATOR (shrugging): Not a word. I only speak Arabic. Speak slower and louder. Maybe they'll understand.

COLUMBUS (giving the translator a dirty look): What a help you are.

(The Chief of the Tainos and six Tainos enter.)

CHIEF: Welcome to our island. Where is yours? (pause) Why all the clothes? (pointing to the sun) Aren't you hot?

TAINO 3 (joking): Maybe they have a skin condition or tails to hide.

(He pinches Rodrigo de Escovedo on the cheek.)

RODRIGO DE ESCOVEDO (rubbing his cheek angrily): Hey!

(De Escovedo pinches the Taino.)

TAINO 3 (rubbing his or her cheek): Hey!

(The Chief and Columbus laugh loudly. Then everyone else laughs, except Rodrigo de Escovedo and Taino 3, but they finally begin to laugh, too. The Tainos and the

sailors proceed to make friends with each other.)

COLUMBUS: De Triana, where is that bag from the Santa Maria?

RODRIGO DE TRIANA (handing Columbus the bag): Here it is, sir.

COLUMBUS (pulls out a bell and some glass beads and hands them to the Chief): Please accept these gifts.

CHIEF (looking at the gifts with curiosity): Thank you. (He takes a fish-bone belt from around his waist and a gold ring from his finger and gives them to Columbus.) And this is for you.

COLUMBUS (can hardly contain himself when he sees the gold ring): You're too kind. (turning to Rodrigo de Triana and whispering excitedly) I told you we would find gold! There's sure to be more where this came from!

SCENE 2: Several months later. On the deck of the Santa Maria.

NARRATOR: Columbus and his men sailed to nearby islands and explored them. He still expected to find the coast of China. Wherever the ships stopped, curious men, women and children came in canoes to exchange gifts.

COLUMBUS: Martin, look at those boats.

MARTIN ALONZO PINZON: What workmanship! Do you see? It looks as if each boat is carved from a single tree! Some of them look big enough to hold 50 people!

(A canoe comes alongside the Santa Maria. Columbus looks down and sees a gold mask in the canoe. He dangles a pair of red shoes over the side and gestures at the canoe. A trade is made: the mask for the shoes.)

COLUMBUS: And the gold! Look at this! (he taps the gold mask and gestures to the people in the canoe) Where did you find this? Do you have more? More—do you have more gold?

ACT 4
★★★★★ SCENE: Several months later on, the coast of Guanahani where the Spaniards originally landed. Columbus and Martin Alonzo Pinzon are on the beach. Spaniards and Taino people are busy loading supplies into canoes to take out to the Spanish ships.

COLUMBUS: Martin, have all the supplies been loaded? The gold is safely on board? I must have it to prove my success to Queen Isabella.

MARTIN ALONZO PINZON: Yes, sir. (looking around.) It will be hard to leave. I'll miss so many people.

COLUMBUS: I want to take some of them back with us. I want to make sure Isabella believes me. Find five or six Indians, willing or not. Do it quietly, just before we leave. We can train them as translators. Now, have you got the volunteers to stay behind and build the fort? With the Santa Maria run aground, the fewer men we have to carry the better.

MARTIN ALONZO PINZON: I got about 40, without much trouble at all. Some of the men want to stay.

(The Chief, accompanied by a crowd of Tainos and Spaniards, enters.)

COLUMBUS (to the Tainos)**:** Good-bye, my friends. I'll be back.

CHIEF: We will take good care of your friends here. Be safe.

COLUMBUS (to the sailors who are staying behind)**:** Good-bye men. Behave well for Spain. (to the rest of the sailors) To our ships!

(The Spaniards depart.)

NARRATOR: Columbus's return to Spain was a success. He took back parrots, gold, and several unwilling Tainos who served as slaves. Although Columbus made three more trips and discovered bigger and more beautiful islands, he never did find the western route to the East Indies. Other Spaniards followed in his path, and the Tainos's home was changed forever.

Christopher Columbus
Teaching Guide

Christopher Columbus was born in Genoa, Italy, in 1451. The details of his life are in dispute. It is believed that he spent his early years as a weaver in his father's business. In 1476, working as a seaman, Columbus was shipwrecked off the coast of Portugal. He eventually made his way to Lisbon where his brother Bartholomew, a highly respected chart maker, lived. At this time, Portugal was in its Golden Age of discovery and exploration. Surrounded by many navigators and explorers who believed in far off islands in the west, Columbus became a master chart maker, navigator, and dreamer. His lifelong quest of reaching the spice-rich East Indies, which he called "Enterprise of the Indies," was born in Lisbon. After a stint as a sugar buyer in the Portuguese islands off Africa, Columbus returned to Lisbon and married Doña Filipa Perestrello. Columbus began to seek help from the Portuguese and the Spanish courts to finance his enterprise, but he was repeatedly rebuffed. At last, after eight years, King Ferdinand and Queen Isabella agreed to back the journey. On August 3, 1492, Columbus set sail for the East Indies. Unfortunately, North and South America (two continents of which the Europeans were unaware) stood in the way. After making four attempts to reach the East Indies, Columbus retired. He died in 1506 a well-off but almost forgotten man.

Book Links

The Log of Christopher Columbus's First Voyage to America: In the Year 1492, As Copied Out in Brief by Bartholomew Las Casas (Linnet Books, 1989)

The Tainos: The People Who Welcomed Columbus by Francine Jacobs (Putnam, 1992)

Columbus and the World Around Him by Milton Meltzer (Franklin Watts, 1990)

EXTENSION ACTIVITIES

Talk About It

☆ **CREDIT OR BLAME?:** Because Columbus believed that he had found the Indies, the native peoples of North and South America were called Indians. On October 12, we celebrate Columbus Day and the "discovery" of America. What impact do students believe that Columbus has had on North America? Do they feel that he deserves credit or blame for his explorations?

Write About It

⭐ **EXPLORER'S LOG:** After reading selections from Columbus's log, imagine that you were on the first voyage. How would it feel to be hungry and thirsty and surrounded by the ocean? How did the sight of land affect you? At first, what did you think of the Taino people? Did your opinion change as you got to know them? Write a log about one part of the expedition.

⭐ **CULTURAL TRADING CARDS:** Major cultural exchanges took place between the Europeans and the Native Americans. The Europeans introduced horses to North and South America. The Native Americans grew crops such as corn, tomatoes, and potatoes that Europeans had never seen. Let students make trading cards for these goods. They should illustrate their cards and write descriptions of the items, explaining their importance and how they may be used. Hold a trading fair where students make trade exchanges.

Report About It

⭐ **TRACING COLUMBUS' ROUTE:** Today Guanahani, or San Salvador, as Columbus called it, is known as Watling Island. It is one of the Bahamas Islands. On a world map, trace the route from Spain to Guanahani. Name and locate the other islands that Columbus is credited with discovering. Research to find the *original* names of these islands. Two examples are Colba, renamed Cuba, and Hispaniola, renamed the Dominican Republic and Haiti. Other islands that Columbus "discovered" include Trinidad, Jamaica, the Virgin Islands, and Puerto Rico.

⭐ **MYTHS AND REALITIES:** Many details about Columbus himself and his journeys are not known. There is still controversy over which island in the Bahamas Columbus and his men first set foot on. Other myths persist. Here are two of the myths:

> **MYTH 1:** *Educated people in the fifteenth century said the world was flat.*
> **REALITY:** *Almost everyone believed the world was round.*
>
> **MYTH 2:** *Columbus was the first European to set foot on the "New World."*
> **REALITY:** *Columbus never set foot on the mainland. The Vikings and perhaps the Phoenicians were the first Europeans to see North and South America; it was Amerigo Vespucci who is credited with the discovery of the continent.*

Send students on a treasure hunt for the truth. Have them choose "facts" about Columbus, his journeys, or the beliefs of people in the 1400s, and then find at least two different sources that either support or dispute those facts.

⭐ **EXPLORING NATURE CULTURES:** Millions of Native Americans with thriving civilizations were living in the southern and northern hemispheres when Columbus arrived. About one million lived in the area known today as the United States. These tribes were the Makah, Hopi, Navajo, Apache, Creek, Chickasaw, Choctaw, Penobscot, Mandan, and Pueblo. Find out more about these early Native Americans. In which parts of North America did these Native Americans live? How did the people gather food? Did they hunt, farm, or fish? What kinds of leisure activities did they enjoy? Find examples of the types of homes each group built and the art they produced. Draw a map of the United States and divide it into northwest, southwest, northeast, and southeast, and place each group in its home territory. If a Navajo woman met a Choctaw woman, could they understand each other? Or did they have to use gestures just as the Tainos and the Spaniards did?

Ben Franklin

Philosopher, Inventor, Community Activist

by Adam Grant

Characters (in order of appearance):

NARRATOR

MRS. FABER

CARLA FABER

MR. FABER

KATRINA FABER

STRANGER/BEN FRANKLIN

WILLIAM: Ben Franklin's son

ACT 1

★★★★★★ SCENE: 1994. The Franklin Institute Science Museum in Philadelphia. The Faber family is looking at the exhibits.

NARRATOR: The year is 1994. Katrina Faber, her sister Carla, and their parents are spending Saturday afternoon at the Franklin Institute Science Museum in Philadelphia.

MRS. FABER: Hey kids, come look at this! It's a whole exhibit on all the things Ben Franklin invented. He was from Philly, you know, just like us.

CARLA: No he wasn't. He was born in Boston.

MRS. FABER: But he lived here in Philadelphia most of his life. This was his favorite city. That's more important than where someone is born, isn't it?

MR. FABER: Wow! This is pretty incredible! Look at all the stuff he invented. Wood stoves . . . bifocals . . .

KATRINA: What are bifocals?

CARLA: Special glasses. The lenses are split across the middle. The top half is for seeing long distances and the bottom half is for reading.

KATRINA: You just read that off the display case. *I* could have done that.

MR. FABER: Old Ben got so tired of having to switch from his regular glasses to his reading glasses that he just combined the two and invented bifocals. Pretty smart, huh?

KATRINA: I guess so. *Not.*

NARRATOR: Katrina sits down on a bench. Her mom and dad and Carla wander off in different directions, looking at the different exhibits.

MRS. FABER: Here's something about Franklin discovering electricity.

NARRATOR: Katrina sees a strange looking man in the corner. He has very little hair and looks pretty old—not to mention the way he's dressed. He's wearing a shiny suit with ruffles at the wrists, and his pants only go down to his knees. His shoes have silver buckles on them. Still, Katrina's sure she's seen him somewhere before.

STRANGER: Never happened.

KATRINA: What?

STRANGER: Never happened. Never discovered electricity.

KATRINA: Hey—who *are* you?

STRANGER: What do you mean? You don't recognize Old Ben? Ben Franklin?

KATRINA: You can't be Ben Franklin, he was born about a million years ago.

FRANKLIN: Young lady, how old is your grandfather?

KATRINA: I don't know . . . 65, maybe.

FRANKLIN: Would you offer him a seat if he were here?

KATRINA: Sure!

FRANKLIN: Well, I'm four times his age, so how about it? Hop up!

(Katrina jumps up from the bench. Ben Franklin sits down and kicks off his shoes.)

KATRINA: Boy, Ben Franklin, right here in front of me. How did you—

FRANKLIN: Never mind. Curiosity killed the cat, you know.

KATRINA: What cat?

FRANKLIN: Oh, brother! Forget it kid, it's just an expression. So where were we? What were we talking about?

KATRINA: Electricity.

FRANKLIN: That's right. Your mother—charming woman—said I discovered it, but that's not quite true. The Greeks discovered electricity almost 3,000 years ago in 600 B.C. Of course, they didn't really know what to do with it. All they knew was that rubbing amber with a piece of wool would create static electricity. The same thing happens when you take your hat off in the winter and your hair stands straight up in the air.

KATRINA: That's electricity?

FRANKLIN: Sure, just like in your TV.

KATRINA: How do you know about TV?

FRANKLIN: I keep up.

KATRINA: Oh. So, if you didn't discover electricity, what did you do?

FRANKLIN: I figured out that lightning was *made* of electricity. Here, I'll show you. Close your eyes for a second.

ACT 2
★★★★★★ **SCENE: 1752. Ben Franklin's home in Philadelphia.**

NARRATOR: When Katrina opens her eyes, she finds herself in the living room of a house. She sees Ben Franklin, with his shoes on, sitting in a chair and talking to a younger man. The young man's pants are too short, and his shoes have silver buckles on them.

FRANKLIN: What are your plans today, son?

WILLIAM: Nothing much. I've got some chores to do.

FRANKLIN: How would you like to help me with an electrical experiment?

WILLIAM: Sure, I guess the chickens can wait.

FRANKLIN: Good! It's going to be a rainy evening—perfect weather for our experiment. Let's get started.

NARRATOR: Katrina watches as they make a kite out of two crossed strips of cedar wood and an old handkerchief. She wonders if they need her help, or if they can even see her.

FRANKLIN: Just think, William, electricity was discovered hundreds of years ago. Yet nobody really knows what it is, or how to use it, or if it *can* be used.

WILLIAM: Is it magic?

FRANKLIN: Not magic. I suspect it comes from nature. Although anything as powerful and mysterious as lightning must have *some* magic in it. My guess is that it's made of electricity. That's what I hope we can prove today.

WILLIAM: How?

FRANKLIN: Metal attracts electricity, and I think it attracts lightning, as well. We'll take this kite and tie a large metal key to it with a string.

NARRATOR: Katrina watches as the two men take the kite outside into the rain. She follows them slowly. Soon they are both soaking wet. Katrina looks down at her own dry clothes and almost misses seeing Ben tie the key to the kite. He holds on to the string as William runs with the kite. The strong wind takes the kite high into the air.

FRANKLIN: William, look for a dark rain cloud and direct me to it.

KATRINA: Hey wait! That's really dangerous! I heard about someone who got hit by lightning on a golf course and got killed! Hey! Can you hear me?

NARRATOR: Ben and his son don't seem to hear Katrina's warning. The lightning crashes all around them, but they keep their eyes on the kite. Finally, Ben signals his son that it's time to stop.

FRANKLIN: Now! I'll simply touch the key with my knuckle. (touching the key) Yeow!

WILLIAM: Did you see that? Did you see that spark fly off that key? Was that electricity? Was that huge spark electricity?

FRANKLIN: It certainly was! We've done it, William! We've proven that lightning is made of electricity!

WILLIAM: How does that help us?

FRANKLIN: Do you remember last summer when those houses burned to the ground after they were hit by lightning? I think we can prevent fires like that.

WILLIAM: How?

FRANKLIN: We know that electricity is attracted to metal, and that lightning usually strikes the tallest thing around. If we put a metal pole next to every house that's taller than the house itself, the lightning will hit the pole instead of the house.

WILLIAM (turning to Katrina): Hey Katrina. It's time to go!

KATRINA: What?

WILLIAM: I said it's time to go!

ACT 3
★★★★★★ SCENE 1: 1994. Franklin Institute Science Museum.

NARRATOR: All of a sudden, Katrina blinks and finds herself sitting on the bench at the Franklin Institute. Katrina's dad is shaking her on the shoulder.

MR. FABER: Hey, Katrina, it's time to go! I said it's time to go! Have you been sleeping on this bench all afternoon?

CARLA: I'll bet you've really learned a *lot*.

KATRINA: Oh yeah? I learned plenty today. For one thing, Ben Franklin didn't discover electricity. The Greeks did that, in 600 B.C. Ben Franklin discovered that lightning was made of electricity, and he used that information to invent the lightning rod.

MRS. FABER: Good for you, Katrina! Where did you learn that?

KATRINA: Ben Franklin told me—I mean—I must have read it somewhere.

CARLA: Read it somewhere? You?

MR. FABER: That's enough, you two. Let's hit the road.

KATRINA: I need to get a drink of water first. I'll hurry.

NARRATOR: As Katrina goes to the water fountain, she sees someone carefully studying the electricity exhibit.

KATRINA: Hey, Mr. Franklin, it's you again. What are you doing?

FRANKLIN: I may be 200 years old, but I've still got things to learn.

22

KATRINA: I told my parents about the lightning rod. That was great.

FRANKLIN: That's nothing, kid. I did a lot of things. I formed the first fire department, established the first free library, invented the wood stove, signed the Declaration of Independence *and* the Constitution. I went to France to raise money for the American Revolution. I was even the first postmaster in America.

KATRINA: Wow, you did all those things? That's amazing! I can't even get all my homework done.

FRANKLIN: Aw, come on, kid. Anybody can accomplish a lot if they believe in themselves and work hard. Nothing is so complicated that we can't understand it. All you have to do is slow down and think it through carefully. Pretty soon it'll make sense to you.

KATRINA: I guess so.

FRANKLIN: You guess so? Look, when I was young there were a million things we didn't understand about science and medicine. But I read everything I could get my hands on and I spent lots of time thinking about things. Try it. You'll be surprised what you discover.

NARRATOR: Ben Franklin pulls a penny from behind Katrina's ear and hands it to her. She looks at him in surprise.

FRANKLIN: Here's a penny for your thoughts.

KATRINA: How'd you do that?

FRANKLIN: Magic.

KATRINA: Thanks, Mr. Franklin. Thanks for everything.

SCENE 2: Later that night. Katrina's bedroom.

(Mrs. Faber comes into Katrina's room to say good night.)

MRS. FABER: I'm glad you had a good time at the museum today. You sure learned a lot.

KATRINA: It was really fun.

(Mrs. Faber sees the shiny penny on Katrina's desk and picks it up.)

MRS. FABER: This penny is from 1789. Where did you get this?

KATRINA (smiling): An "old" friend gave it to me.

Ben Franklin
Teaching Guide

Ben Franklin was born in Boston in 1700. As a young man he was devoted to reading—a rare and impractical trait for a boy of his time. He worked for a while in his father's candle shop and then as an apprentice in his brother James' print shop. Soon, Franklin found his way to Philadelphia, where he met and married Deborah Read. He soon became a successful printer and newspaper editor. In 1732, Franklin began to publish *Poor Richard's Almanac*, a calendar and weather forecast for the year, with jokes, homilies, and words of wisdom. He also began to invent things and to explore science. Among his inventions were the wood stove, the battery, bifocal glasses, and the lightning rod. His community work in Philadelphia led him to establish the first free library in the colonies, as well as the first volunteer fire department. He also helped to found the University of Pennsylvania. Franklin's genius was not limited to one field; he excelled as a philosopher, printer, inventor, scientist, and statesman. His signature appears on both the Declaration of Independence and the United States Constitution. In 1789, he signed a petition to the first United States Congress calling for an end to slavery. He died that same year at the age of 89.

Book Links

The Story of Ben Franklin: Amazing American by Margaret Davidson (Dell Publishing Company, 1988)

Benjamin Franklin: Man of Science by Irmengarde Eberle (Franklin Watts, Inc., 1961)

Benjamin Franklin by Robin McKown (G.P. Putnam's Sons, 1963)

The Autobiography of Benjamin Franklin with an introduction by J.W. Bigoness (Airmont, 1965)

EXTENSION ACTIVITIES

Talk About It

☆ **FAVORITE MUSEUMS:** The setting of the play is the Franklin Institute Science Museum in Philadelphia. Have any of your students visited that museum? If so, ask them to tell the rest of the class what it was like. Discuss other museums students have visited. Which were their favorites and why? Point out the different kinds of museums mentioned. Ask students to talk about why museums are important and how they help us.

☆ **LOCAL LIGHT AND POWER:** Thanks to Ben Franklin and his kite and key, we learned more about electricity and its potential. How is the electricity for your community generated? If possible, arrange a trip to a local power plant. Before the trip, guide students in formulating a list of questions they'd like to ask at the plant. As an alternate, you may wish to invite an electrician to speak to the class. Ask her or him to point out how some of the things people do every day depend upon electricity, such as using the telephone. Afterwards, have students imagine what their lives would be like without electricity. How would their daily activities change?

Write About It

☆ **CLASS ALMANAC:** *Poor Richard's Almanac* contained information about the weather, as well as jokes and homilies. If possible, bring in a copy of Franklin's almanac. Discuss the idea of "homegrown philosophy," and how common sense and good humor can be important and useful in our lives. Have each member of the class write a few of their own homilies such as "early to bed, early to rise" and incorporate them into a class almanac. Start each school day by letting a volunteer read a homily or write it on the chalkboard.

☆ **PUT ON A PLAY:** In addition to being an inventor, Franklin was a political activist and statesman. Ask students to use information discovered in the research activity below to write their own play about Benjamin Franklin. They may decide to form a group to work on each act, or they may wish to write independently.

Report About It

☆ **THE CAMPAIGN TRAIL, 1788:** Ben Franklin, George Washington, and Thomas Jefferson were all influential in the creation of the United States. As the first president, Washington didn't have to run against anybody. What might have happened if the three men had run against each other in a presidential campaign? Divide the class into three groups. Each group should focus on one of the men. What presidential qualities does each have? What kinds of experience do they have that indicate they would be capable of governing? Then they should present their subjects as if each man were running for president. After the presentations, hold an election.

☆ **BEN FRANKLIN DOCUDRAMA:** When did Franklin invent the wood stove? How did he become the first postmaster of the United States? How did he have time to accomplish all that he did? Ask students to imagine that Ben Franklin was going to visit your class. Have them do research on his achievements and then prepare a "This Is Your Life, Ben Franklin" book, video, or oral presentation. Invite the principal or another adult to play the role of Ben Franklin.

George Washington
A Soldier, a Peaceful Man

by James Aley

Characters (in order of appearance):

NARRATORS 1-2
LAWRENCE WASHINGTON: George's brother
LORD FAIRFAX
GEORGE WASHINGTON
FRENCH COMMANDER
MARTHA WASHINGTON
DINNER GUESTS 1-5
SOLDIERS 1-3

ACT 1

★★★★★ SCENE: 1748. George Washington and his brother Lawrence have joined Lord Fairfax on the grounds of Fairfax's large estate.

NARRATOR 1: The colonists in America are eager to explore the continent. Many want to move west and build new homes and farms. One wealthy colonist, Lord Fairfax, owns over five million acres of land. Much of that land remains unexplored.

NARRATOR 2: Fairfax's friend, Lawrence Washington, suggests a person to survey the land: his sixteen-year-old brother George. Lawrence assures Lord Fairfax that George is disciplined, responsible, and a whiz in math.

LAWRENCE: Good morning, Lord Fairfax. I'd like you to meet my brother George.

LORD FAIRFAX: Glad to meet to you, George. Lawrence tells me you're a wonderful young man. Good in math, are you?

GEORGE: I like working with numbers, sir.

LORD FAIRFAX: Lawrence also says you're about the most honest person he knows. Isn't there a story that you cut down a cherry tree and then admitted to your father that you did it?

GEORGE: I cannot tell a lie, sir. That story is not true.

LORD FAIRFAX (laughing): You are honest, aren't you, son! Now—I own five million acres of land, but it's mostly untamed wilderness. I don't even have a map of it. I've talked with your brother about this, and I trust his judgment. He tells me I should trust yours. Knowing your family, I'm inclined to believe him. I want to hire you to survey and map my land west of the Blue Ridge Mountains.

GEORGE: I'd be honored, sir. I won't disappoint you.

LORD FAIRFAX: It'll be a tough job. It'll mean harsh living—cold and wet. You won't have doctors to help you if you get sick or you hurt yourself. You'll be on your own, with only your wits to guide you.

GEORGE: You can count on me, Lord Fairfax. I'll be fine.

ACT 2

★★★★★ SCENE: 1754. The cabin of the French commander at Fort Duquesne on the Ohio River.

NARRATOR 1: Washington's next job was to convince the French to move out of the Ohio Valley. The governor of Virginia sent Washington to Fort Duquesne with a letter demanding that the French leave the territory.

NARRATOR 2: England and France were both claiming the same land along the Ohio River. France had built several forts there, and French trappers and soldiers were moving into the area.

(Washington knocks and then enters the cabin.)

WASHINGTON: The governor of Virginia sends his greetings.

(He hands the commander a letter from the governor.)

COMMANDER: I believe I know what your governor wants. He wants to take possession of French lands.

WASHINGTON: The surveys clearly show that I am standing on English ground.

COMMANDER: Lines can be drawn anywhere on a map. My surveys show that this is French land.

WASHINGTON: Then with your permission, I'd like to re-survey the area myself.

COMMANDER: I think I know what your "survey" would show.

WASHINGTON: It would show who the true owner of the territory is—whether it favors the English or the French.

COMMANDER: This is French territory. We are here, and we will fight to keep it. Is there anything else?

WASHINGTON: You may be here, but this territory is not yours.

NARRATOR 1: After the interview, Washington with 150 men attacked a French scouting party. Ten of the French were killed. The Virginians then built a small fort, Fort Necessity, on low ground. Heavy rains came and ruined their gunpowder. When the French retaliated, they easily defeated the Virginians. Washington escaped unharmed.

NARRATOR 2: The next year, in 1755, Washington returned to the area as part of General Braddock's army. The French and Indian War—a fight between the French and the British—had begun. In one battle, Washington collected four bullet holes in his coat and had two horses shot from underneath him, but again he escaped unharmed. The fighting lasted until 1760 when the French admitted defeat.

ACT 3
★★★★★ **SCENE: The 1770s. Mount Vernon, the Washington's home in Virginia. Martha and George Washington are hosting a dinner party.**

NARRATOR 1: After the French were defeated, Washington went back home to his family's estate, Mount Vernon, in Virginia. He married Martha Dandridge

28

Custis, a widow with two small children, and settled down to a quiet but productive life as a farmer.

NARRATOR 2: It wasn't always quiet at Mount Vernon. George and Martha liked to invite guests to their home. Their dinner parties were filled with lively talk. Life in the colonies hadn't calmed down after the French and Indian War. The English expected the colonists to help pay for the war. By the 1770s, the colonists were angered by the taxes England had slapped on them. Many people expected war, and they wanted George Washington to lead the fight.

GUEST 1: The King taxes lead, glass, paper, paint, and tea; we say "Fine! We won't buy those products from England." The English merchants scream and shout, and the King says, "Well, how about we just tax the tea a little?"

GUEST 2: Don't drink it, I say. I like coffee better, anyway.

GUEST 3: That's not the point! How can they expect us to pay taxes when we can't even elect anyone to the British Parliament!

GUEST 4: That's right! There's no one to stand up for us!

GUEST 5: Mark my words—we're heading for a fight. We need someone to lead it.

GEORGE: We don't need another war. I agree that these actions by the British are an outrage, but we mustn't go to war unless every other plan has failed.

MARTHA: George and I have promised to support a boycott of British goods. We won't allow any taxed products into this house. But I don't think that's enough. The British are treating us badly. We do need someone to set them straight.

GUEST 1: They won't stop taxing us. They won't let us into Parliament. What should we do? Just keep telling King George that he's not being very nice to us?

GEORGE: If we've tried all peaceful means—then, and only then, should we even consider war.

ACT 4
★★★★★ **SCENE: 1777. Washington's quarters in Valley Forge, Pennsylvania. It is a bitter cold December evening. Washington is looking over maps and stamping his feet to keep warm.**

NARRATOR 1: The colonists did try every plan and the British wouldn't listen. Finally, the colonists formed a special group, the Continental Congress, to discuss what to do. Each colony sent representatives to Philadelphia in 1774. The Continental Congress made Washington commander of the militias of all the colonies. On July 4, 1776, the Congress signed the Declaration of Independence. They declared that America was no longer part of Britain. The Revolutionary War had begun.

NARRATOR 2: With little money or supplies, Washington made a ragtag group of men into an army. His men were often cold, wet, and sick, but they had great respect for General Washington. In the bitter winter of 1777, Washington and his troops camped in Valley Forge, near Philadelphia. He had his men build cabins so they could stay as warm and safe as possible.

SOLDIER 1: This note just came for you, sir. It's from the Pennsylvania government.

GEORGE: Thank you, soldier. (As Washington reads the letter, he grows angry.) What? They think we're spending too much money? They think it would be cheaper if the men would stay out in the field and not in cabins? This is ridiculous! And they want us to use fewer supplies? Who do they think they are? They're sitting snugly in their homes while these men are fighting for their freedom! Nonsense! My men deserve more blankets and medicine, not less! (to the soldier) Send a letter back to these . . . idiots. Tell them we want more blankets, more medicine, more shoes, more hats, and less complaining. Got that?

SOLDIER 1 (writing and smiling): Yes, General. I'll deliver it right away.

(Soldier leaves Washington's office, goes outside where other soldiers are waiting.)

SOLDIER 2: Well, what did he say?

SOLDIER 1: The General told them to send more supplies.

SOLDIER 3: I hope for his sake we win this war. He sure knows how we're all suffering.

ACT 5
★ ★ ★ ★ ★ ★ SCENE: 1797. New York City, the nation's capital. Washington is on a stage in front of a podium, preparing to give his last speech as President of the United States.

NARRATOR 1: After eight years of fighting, Washington led his troops to victory. The colonies were no longer colonies, but they weren't yet a nation, either. America needed a strong government to hold the country together. The Constitution was adopted, and the United States of America was born. Washington became the first President of the United States. In the spring of 1789, he left his home for New York City, then the capital, to take the oath of office.

NARRATOR 2: Washington was as successful a president as he was a general. He organized the first cabinet, or group of leaders, to help him run the country. As president, he kept the country together during its first difficult years. In 1796, before the end of his second term, Washington wrote his farewell address, one of the most important documents in American history. He asked Americans to stick together and accept the challenges of their new form of government.

WASHINGTON (reading his speech): Friends and Fellow Citizens, the time for you to choose a new president is near. I am retiring for good from public life. But before I go, I want to leave you with some thoughts I have had as your president. The name "American," which belongs to you, must always show the just pride of patriotism, more than any other name. You're all different, but not so different that you cannot work out your problems. You have fought for a common cause and triumphed together. The independence and liberty you possess are the work of all of you; of your common dangers, sufferings and successes.

George Washington
Teaching Guide

George Washington was born on February 11, 1732, at his family's home at Bridges Creek, Virginia. Not much is known about his childhood, but there is no evidence of his chopping down a cherry tree and admitting to the deed later. Washington did, however, write a list of "Rules of Civility" when he was 15 years old, a list he adhered to throughout his life. By the age of 23, he was in command of the entire militia of the state of Virginia. In 1759 Washington married Martha Dandridge Custis, a young widow with two children, Martha and John. During his private years, Washington gained a reputation as a farmer, and he introduced many scientific methods to agriculture. In 1775, the Continental Congress appointed Washington commander of American forces. After winning the war in 1783, Washington again retired to Mount Vernon. Although retired, he remained active in the development and signing of the new Constitution. In gratitude for his military and political leadership, the new nation made him president in 1788. Washington's presidency was distinguished by his cool-headedness in the face of political turmoil at home in the new United States and overseas in Europe. He retired from public life for the last time in 1797. George Washington died in 1799.

Book Links

George Washington: Man & Monument by Marcus Cunliffe (American Library, 1984)

The World of Young George Washington by Suzanne Hilton (Walker & Co., 1987)

George Washington and the Birth of Our Nation by Milton Meltzer (Watts, 1986)

EXTENSION ACTIVITIES

Talk About It

★ **UNITED STATES OF ENGLAND!:** King George III was the King of England at the time of the American Revolution. Encourage students to talk about what they know about Queen Elizabeth II and her duties. Ask the students if they can explain the differences between a president and a monarch. List their ideas on the blackboard. After comparing and contrasting the two roles, initiate a discussion about what might have happened if the British had won the Revolutionary War. How would our lives today be different?

⭐ **MOUNT VERNON-STYLE DEBATE:** Martha and George Washington liked to entertain at Mount Vernon. People with different ideas probably sat at the same table. Hold your own Mount Vernon dinner party. Divide the class into three groups: pro-British, anti-British, and those who agree with Washington's more peaceful approach, and then let the debate begin.

Write About It

⭐ **RULES OF CIVILITY:** George Washington wrote down a list of "Rules of Civility," or rules about how one should live, when he was only 15 years old. Some of his rules are listed below:

> "It is better to be alone than in bad company."
> "Do not be curious about other people's business."
> "Do not say bad things about people behind their backs."
> "Keep your nails clean and short."
> "Do not eat in the street, nor in your house, out of season."

Some of Washington's rules seem more practical today than others do. Still, he took the rules seriously and lived by them. Ask student to write their own rules of civility. Compile the lists to create your own set of rules to use in the classroom.

⭐ **SOLDIERS' LETTERS:** Washington suffered along with his men at Valley Forge. Ask students to imagine themselves in the shoes of the soldier who delivered the Pennsylvania Government's message to Washington. How would he have written about the incident in a journal or a letter home? Encourage them to consider some of the following questions: What are the soldier's feelings about Washington? Does he believe that the colonies will win the war? What is the night like, the weather outside? What does he miss most about home?

Be sure to give students opportunities to share their writing via read-alouds, bulletin boards, writing walls, learning centers, and so on.

Report About It

⭐ **MOVING SPEECHES:** The Farewell Address that Washington delivered is one of the most famous documents in American history because it helped the American people accept a strong union of states. Ask the students if they can name some other famous documents and speeches, for example, Martin Luther King's "I Have a Dream" speech and Abraham Lincoln's Gettysburg Address. Guide students in researching other speeches that have influenced Americans, such as speeches by John F. Kennedy, Toni Morrison, Cesar Chavez, or Barbara Jordan. Ask them to select a speech that personally moves them and then find out how it affected the country. If students wish, they may read the speech aloud and share with the class what it means to them.

⭐ **COMPARING BATTLE TACTICS:** Washington learned a great deal about military strategy when he fought in the French and Indian War. What he learned helped him to defeat the British in the Revolutionary War. Ask students to research the differences in the way in the which the French and Native Americans fought and how Washington later incorporated their strategies into his battle plans during the Revolutionary War. Some students may wish to use maps and diagrams or dioramas and scale models to present their findings, while others may focus on a particular individual such as Sir William Warraghiyagey Johnson or Louis Montcalm. Encourage students to look at letters and diaries of the time to get a feeling for what the French and Indian War was like.

Phillis Wheatley
Voice of Freedom

by Timothy Nolan

Characters (in order of appearance):

READER
NARRATORS 1-2
PHILLIS WHEATLEY
PHILLIS' FATHER
AUCTIONEER
JOHN WHEATLEY
SUSANNAH WHEATLEY
MARY WHEATLEY
TOWN CRIER
GOVERNOR HUTCHINSON
JOHN HANCOCK
CLERGYMEN 1-3
COUNTESS OF HUNTINGDON
SERVANT (nonspeaking role)

ACT 1

★★★★★★ SCENE: 1761. A crowded market place in Boston.

READER: I, young in life, by seeming cruel fate
Was snatched from Africa's fancied happy seat;
What pangs excruciating must molest,
What sorrows labour in my parent's breast?
Steeled was that soul and by no misery moved,
That from a father seized his babe beloved:
Such, such my case. And can I then but pray
Others may never feel tyrannic sway?

NARRATOR 1: From the 1600's until 1865, ships sailed from America to Africa. The ships returned, filled with enslaved Africans to serve the American colonists. These Africans were taken from their homes, and their families, to a strange place where they became the property of other men. Along with her father, Phillis Wheatley was kidnapped from her home in Senegal, West Africa, when she was about seven or eight years old.

NARRATOR 2: Phillis and her father were brought to Boston, Massachusetts, on the same ship. The trip took months. They were fed nothing but rice and water. Sick, hungry, and very scared, the Africans were taken to a slave auction where they were sold to the wealthy people of Boston. Phillis was separated from her father.

AUCTIONEER: Next! Bring up the next one! Move! Move! Time is money!

(Phillis' father is being forced toward the platform where the auctioneer is standing.)

PHILLIS' FATHER: No! No! Together! She's my little girl—my daughter—

(Phillis is held back as she tries to run after her father. Tears run down her face, but she doesn't say anything.)

AUCTIONEER: You all know how it is—they're upset at first, but they calm down. Take a good look at this one: big and strong. He'll calm down. They always do. What'll you give me for him?

PHILLIS' FATHER: No! I am not alone! We go together!

AUCTIONEER: Twenty-five, give me twenty-five! Thirty, give me thirty! Thirty-five, thirty-five—sold—one big, strong man! Next!

(Phillis is led to the platform. The auctioneer looks her up and down and sighs.)

AUCTIONEER: She's small now, but she'll grow! They always do! Five, who'll give me five? Five, I'll take five. Who'll give me five?

JOHN WHEATLEY: I will. I'll give you five.

ACT 2
★★★★★ **SCENE:** *1766. The large and comfortable home of John and Susannah Wheatley in Boston, Massachusetts.*

NARRATOR 1: Phillis was taken to the Wheatley home. She took care of John Wheatley's wife Susannah and helped with other household and kitchen chores. The Wheatley's daughter Mary taught Phillis to read and write. Mary's twin brother Nathaniel gave Phillis lessons in Latin and science. Phillis was often ill and unable to work. It was during these times that she began to write poetry.

NARRATOR 2: In May of 1766, just before dawn, all the bells in Boston started to ring. Everyone in the Wheatley household jumped out of bed and hurried to their windows. They heard the town crier shouting in the distance.

MARY: Can you hear what he's saying, Phillis?

PHILLIS (shaking her head): I can't make it out.

MARY: What can it be? Oh, I hope it's not bad news!

PHILLIS: There go Mr. Wheatley and Nathaniel to find out what's happening.

MARY: I hope they don't go far!

PHILLIS: Listen, Miss Mary. Did you make that out?

TOWN CRIER: The Stamp Act is dead! The Stamp Act is dead! Long live the king! The Stamp Act is dead! The Stamp Act is dead! Long live the king!

MARY: Thank goodness—good news! No more taxes on our newspapers and books. Just think, Phillis, the king backed down.

PHILLIS: Maybe he's a friend to us after all.

MARY: I hope so. Oh, I hope so! Here come father and Nathaniel. I'll see if they have more news.

NARRATOR 1: Phillis went to her desk. She sat down, picked up her pen, and wrote a poem to King George III.

READER: Your subjects hope, dread Sire,
            The crown upon your brows
            may flourish long,
            And that your arm may in your God
            be strong! . . .
            Sometimes by Simile's a victory won

A certain lady had an only son...
She laid some taxes on her darling son
And would have laid another act there on...
He wept, Britannia turned a senseless ear,
At last awaken'd by maternal fear...
He weeps afresh this Iron chain
Turn, O Britannia claim the child again...
To raise their own Profusion, O Britain see
By this New England will increase like thee.

ACT 3

★★★★★ SCENE: 1772. The home of Governor Hutchinson. Phillis is surrounded by Mr. Wheatley, Governor Hutchinson, John Hancock, clergymen, and government officials.

NARRATOR 1: When Mary Wheatley got married, Phillis wrote a poem as a wedding gift. Mary asked her to read the poem at the wedding. Some people found it hard to believe that Phillis could be a poet. One publisher told Mary that slaves couldn't write poetry and refused to publish Phillis' poems. The Wheatleys arranged for a test that would prove that Phillis could be—and was—a poet.

NARRATOR 2: One afternoon Phillis and the Wheatleys went to the mansion of Governor Hutchinson. They were shown into a room. Governor Hutchinson, John Hancock, and fourteen other respected Boston men were already in the room.

GOVERNOR HUTCHINSON: Gentleman, you know why we are here. You may ask Phillis any question you like.

JOHN HANCOCK: I'm ready. Are you prepared to answer our questions, Phillis?

PHILLIS: Yes, sir.

CLERGYMAN 1: Are you a Christian? Have you been baptized?

PHILLIS: I am a member of and attend Old South Church, sir.

(The men look at each other in surprise.)

CLERGYMAN 2: Phillis, would you read something out of the Bible? I have a page marked here.

PHILLIS: Certainly, sir. (She takes the Bible and opens it.) "A false witness shall not be unpunished, and he that speaketh lies shall not escape." Proverbs 19: 5.

CLERGYMAN 3: Do you understand what that means?

PHILLIS: Yes, sir. It's wrong to lie. If you lie, you'll be punished.

38

HANCOCK (to the clergymen): Well, gentleman, I'd say she knows the Bible. I understand you know Latin, Phillis? Is that true?

PHILLIS: Yes, sir.

HANCOCK: Would you mind reciting one of your poems for us?

NARRATOR 1: After Phillis recited her poetry, the sixteen men agreed that Phillis had the education and mind to be a poet.

NARRATOR 2: As proof, they made and signed a statement. Phillis left the room and met Mrs. Wheatley in the hall of the governor's mansion.

MRS. WHEATLEY: What did they say?

PHILLIS (reading the statement): "We, whose names are underwritten, do assure the World that the following pages, were (as we verily believe) written by Phillis, a young Negro girl, who was but a few years since brought an uncultivated barbarian, from Africa . . ."

ACT 4
★★★★★ SCENE: 1773. The Countess of Huntingdon's castle in England.

NARRATOR 1: Phillis Wheatley's first book of poetry was published in England. She had written a poem after the death of one of Mary's friends. The Countess of Huntingdon saw a copy of the poem. She invited Phillis to visit her in England.

COUNTESS: So many people want to meet you, Phillis. Everyone in London is crazy about your book. Lord Dartmouth says people are stopping him on the street and begging him to invite them to your party.

PHILLIS: It's been wonderful being here. You've been so kind.

COUNTESS: I know you miss the Wheatleys, but I do hope you'll stay a little longer. Long enough to meet the king.

PHILLIS: The king?! I couldn't—what would I say?

COUNTESS: Don't worry. He may be the king, but he's not the smartest king we've ever had.

(They are interrupted by a servant. He brings in a tray of letters and sets it beside the Countess. She goes through the letters and hands several to Phillis.)

COUNTESS: You see, Phillis. You get more mail than I do!

PHILLIS (opening letter and reading it): Oh, no!

COUNTESS: What is it?

PHILLIS: It's Mrs. Wheatley. She's dying! Please, Countess, I want to go back. I hope it's not too late.

NARRATOR 2: Phillis returned to Boston. For a while, Mrs. Wheatley seemed to get better. Then, she fell ill again and died. Phillis took charge of the Wheatley household. She had little time for poetry.

ACT 5
★★★★★ **SCENE 1: 1775. General Washington's headquarters. Washington is sitting behind his desk.**

NARRATOR 1: In 1775, the American colonies and England were at war. Red-coated soldiers were camped in Boston. The people of Boston had lived through the Boston Tea Party, the Boston Massacre, the battles of Lexington and Concord, and the battles of Bunker and Breed's Hill.

NARRATOR 2: Just as it seemed the British had control of Boston, Washington marched to Boston. Phillis wrote him a poem. Mary's husband arranged for it to be delivered to Washington.

WASHINGTON: "Thee, first in peace and honours,—we demand
The grace and glory of thy martial band
Fam'd for thy valour, for thy virtues more,
Hear every tongue thy guardian aid implore!
Proceed, great chief, with virtue on thy side,
Thy ev'ry action let the goodness guide.
A crown, a mansion, and a throne that shine
With gold unfading, WASHINGTON! by thine."

(He picks up a pen and begins to write Phyllis a letter.)

SCENE 2: 1776. The Wheatley home. Phillis and Mary are reading a letter that has just been delivered.

MARY: It's from General Washington! Hurry and open it, Phillis! What does he say?

PHILLIS: "Miss Phillis: Your favor of the 26th of October did not reach my hands till the middle of December. Time enough, you will say to have given an answer ere this. Granted. But a variety of important occurrences continually interposing to distract the mind and withdraw the attention, I hope will apologize for the delay and plead my excuse for the seeming neglect. I thank you most sincerely for your polite notice of me in your elegant lines. However undeserving I may be of such encomium and panegyric, the style and manner exhibit a striking proof of your poetical talents. As a tribute justly due to you I would have published the poem had I not been apprehensive that while I only meant to give the world this new instance of your genius, I might have incurred the imputation of vanity. This, and nothing else, determined me not to give it place in the public prints. If you should come to Cambridge or near headquarters I shall be happy to see a person so favored by the Muses, to whom Nature has been so liberal and beneficent in her dispensations. I am, with great respect, Your obedient humble servant. George Washington"

NARRATOR 1: Thanks to the efforts of Thomas Paine, Phillis' poem and Washington's letter were published together in the *Pennsylvania Magazine* in April of 1776.

Phillis Wheatley
Teaching Guide

Phillis Wheatley was born in Senegal, West Africa. In 1761, at about the age of seven or eight, she was brought with her father to Boston on a ship named *Phillis*. She and her father were sold into slavery separately. Phillis was bought by John Wheatley; she never saw her father again. At about the age of thirteen, she began to write poetry in response to personal and public events. Phillis Wheatley traveled to England at the request of the Countess of Huntingdon, who also had Phillis' first book of poetry published in that country. The illness of Susannah Wheatley, John Wheatley's wife, precipitated Phillis' return to Boston before she was due to be presented to King George III. Mrs. Wheatley rallied but died soon after Phillis returned. The Revolutionary War began, and hard times fell on Boston. Phillis was given her freedom by the Wheatleys in 1775. Also in that year, she wrote her famous poem to George Washington and met John Peters, a free man whom she would marry three years later. Phillis and John had three children, two of whom died when they were young. Although he attempted to start his own business, John Peters was jailed for nonpayment of debts. John and Mary Wheatley had both passed away; Nathaniel Wheatley was away in England and unaware of Phillis' plight. Days away from eviction from a boarding house, Phillis Wheatley and her young baby died on December 5, 1784.

Book Links

The Story of Phillis Wheatley: Poetess of the American Revolution by Shirley Graham (Julian Messner, 1969)

Phillis Wheatley by Victoria Sherrow (Chelsea House, 1992)

The Collected Works of Phillis Wheatley ed. by John Shields (Oxford University Press, 1988)

EXTENSION ACTIVITIES

Talk About It

⭐ **INDEPENDENCE FOR ALL?:** The Wheatley's freed Phillis Wheatley in 1775. Many enslaved Africans believed that the War for Independence would mean their freedom, too. What do they think about the fact that white Americans fought for their own freedom and founded a country on the premise that all men are created equal but neglected to abolish slavery?

☆ **WEIGHING PHILLIS' CHOICE:** The life Phillis led in England was much different than the one she led in America. She was a published, well-respected poet invited to meet the King of England. Ask students to think about how Phillis Wheatley's life might have been different if she had stayed in England. Were they surprised that she would want to return to be with Susannah Wheatley? Do they understand why Phillis Wheatley made her choice? What would they have done in her position?

Write About It

☆ **INTERVIEWING PHILLIS:** It took a written statement signed by eighteen prominent men in Boston to prove that Phillis Wheatley was a poet. Too bad they didn't use the meeting to ask Phillis about how she writes poetry. Maybe they would have learned something! Ask students to prepare a list of questions that they would have liked to ask Phillis about her life and her poetry. Then have pairs of students switch questions with each other and provide the answers they feel Phillis Wheatley would have given. Afterward, discuss how asking and answering the questions made them feel.

☆ **DEAR PRESIDENT LETTERS:** Phillis Wheatley often addressed her poetry to a particular person such as King George or George Washington. Encourage students to express themselves in poetry to the President. They may wish to air their own particular concerns, compliment or criticize the President's job performance, or talk about how they feel about their country and/or their futures. Suggest that students bind the poems into a book and send a copy to the President.

Be sure to give students opportunities to share their writing via read-alouds, bulletin boards, writing walls, learning centers, and so on.

Report About It

☆ **LEARNING A POETS' LANGUAGE:** Students may have difficulty in understanding the language and rhythm of Phillis Wheatley's poetry. Explain that poetry in the 18th century usually followed this form. Bring in other examples of Phillis Wheatley's work and the work of her contemporaries, such as Lucy Terry and Philip Freneau. What do these poets tell about life in New England in the 1700s? What do Phillis Wheatley's poems say about the kind of person she was? After discussing the poets and their poems, introduce students to other American poets such as Robert Frost, Langston Hughes, Marianne Moore, and Nikki Giovanni. Ask students to choose one of these poets, or another poet, if they like, and prepare a report based on some of the following questions: How does his or her work differ from Phillis'? How is it similar? What does this poetry say not only about the poet but about the times in which he or she wrote or writes?

⭐ **SING THE UNSUNG HEROS:** About 5,000 African American men and boys fought in the Revolutionary War. Crispus Attucks was the first man shot down in the Boston Massacre; Salem Poor took part in the battle of Breed's Hill; James Forten was a powder boy on the *Royal Louis*. Ask students to find out more about one of these men or another to explore the policies of the Continental Army regarding black soldiers. You also may wish to suggest that students examine how the individual states handled the question of black soldiers in the army.

Meriwether Lewis and William Clark

Their Excellent Adventure

by Justin Martin

Characters (in order of appearance):

NARRATORS 1-2

MERIWETHER LEWIS: Co-captain of expedition;
skilled in botany, zoology, and other sciences

WILLIAM CLARK: Other co-captain; skilled navigator;
excellent at talking with Indians

SACAGAWEA: Shoshone woman; served as guide to Lewis and Clark

CAMEAHWAIT: Sacagawea's brother; a Shoshone chief

GEORGE DREWYER: the expedition's most skilled hunter

PRIVATE PETER CRUZATTE: Crewman

PRIVATE REUBEN FIELDS: Crewman

PRIVATE SILAS GOODRICH: Crewman

ST. LOUIS NEWSPAPER REPORTERS 1-2

ST. LOUIS TOWNSPEOPLE 1-3

ACT 1
★★★★★★ SCENE: 1804. A campsite beside the Missouri River.

NARRATOR 1: In 1803, the United States purchased the Louisiana Territory from France. The Louisiana Purchase added over 800,000 square miles of land to the United States. The purchase doubled the size of the country. The area included all or part of thirteen present-day states, such as Iowa, Kansas, and Missouri. In 1804, President Thomas Jefferson sent Captains Meriwether Lewis and William Clark, along with a crew of skilled boatmen, hunters, and soldiers, to explore the new territory. Their mission was to map the region, observe the plants and wildlife, learn the customs of the Indians, and try to find a river route from the Atlantic to the Pacific Oceans.

NARRATOR 2: We join the expedition now as they pitch camp on the banks of the Missouri River in what is today South Dakota. The date is late September of 1804. After a long day traveling on the river, the crew has gathered around the campfire to discuss the day's events.

CLARK (working on his map as he speaks): I estimate that we traveled 12 miles on the Missouri today. Right here, at about the halfway point, Reuben Fields spotted a creek flowing off to the east. We'll name it Reuben Creek in his honor. And about two miles back, you may remember, we passed a small island in the river. A good day's travel—right?

CRUZATTE, FIELDS, and GOODRICH: Right!

CLARK: Everyone's in a good humor?

CRUZATTE, FIELDS, and GOODRICH: Right!

CLARK: Then we'll call this Good Humored Island.

LEWIS (opening up his journal and preparing to take notes): What about wildlife? Did anyone spot any unusual animals today?

DREWYER: I hiked a little ways inland and spotted a herd of buffalo. Didn't hit any. I got five elk, though. Looks like we're having elk for dinner tomorrow and the day after that—and the day after *that.*

FIELDS: I was walking in an open patch of land and I spotted a whole colony of barking squirrels—funny little animals, standing on their hind legs and chattering—must have been thousands of them.

CRUZATTE (excitedly): I saw this one critter! Like a beaver in shape and size, his head and mouth were like a dog, with short ears, his—his—

LEWIS: Slow down, Peter.

CRUZATTE (still excited): His tail and hair was like a groundhog, but longer, and

46

lighter colored. His skin was thick and loose. His belly was white and—uh—uh—he had a white streak running from his nose to his shoulders. I think he was some kind of small bear.

LEWIS: Sounds like the animal you saw might be what the French call a *brarow*.

CLARK: Or what the Pawnee Indians call a *cho car tooch*.

LEWIS: Anyone else spot any unusual wildlife? What about you, Silas?

GOODRICH (scratching himself): Nothing but these pesky 'skeeters.

NARRATOR 1: The members of the Lewis and Clark expedition were among the very first Americans to encounter many new and interesting animals. The barking squirrels Reuben Fields saw, are what we now know as prairie dogs.

NARRATOR 2: And the animal that got Peter Cruzatte so excited, known to French trappers as a *brarow* and the Pawnees as a *cho car tooch*, was a badger. The pesky 'skeeters bothering Silas Goodrich were, of course, pesky mosquitoes.

ACT 2
★★★★★ SCENE: 1805. The tent of Shoshone chief Cameahwait

NARRATOR 1: By October, Lewis and Clark had journeyed into what is today North Dakota. There they met a Shoshone woman named Sacagawea and her husband Toussaint Charbonneau, a French-Canadian trader. Knowing that Sacagawea could help them meet with Indians, Lewis and Clark asked the couple to join the expedition.

NARRATOR 2: We now join Lewis and Clark in April of 1805 in present-day Montana. Sacagawea has run into people of her own tribe, the Lemhi Shoshone. Her brother Cameahwait is their chief. Lewis and Clark are meeting with Cameahwait. Sacagawea is serving as a translator between her brother and Lewis and Clark.

CAMEAHWAIT (to Sacagawea): We must begin this visit in a civilized fashion.

SACAGAWEA (to Lewis and Clark): My brother would like you to smoke a peace pipe with him.

LEWIS (taking the pipe): Thank you. Sacagawea, tell your brother that we are very honored.

CLARK (handing Sacagawea a medallion with a picture of Thomas Jefferson): Will you give this to Cameahwait and tell him that this is the chief of our nation? Our chief wishes to send his greetings.

CAMEAHWAIT (accepting the medallion and smiling): Tell Mr. Lewis and Mr. Clark that their whole crew is invited to a dance tonight.

SACAGAWEA (to Cameahwait): I warn you—these people dance very strangely. One of them whose name is Silas Goodrich leaps around like a fox cub chasing his own tail. The whole time, he plays some sort of music with a stick. Back and forth, back and forth. It's very funny. Everyone will enjoy it.

CAMEAHWAIT (looking at medallion): Do they think we're as funny?

SACAGAWEA: Oh, yes.

ACT 3
★★★★★ **SCENE: 1806. The banks of the Mississippi River outside of St. Louis, Missouri**

NARRATOR 1: Lewis and Clark traveled on, from Montana into the Oregon Territory and all the way to the Pacific Ocean. Then, their mission completed, they headed back. Along the way, Sacagawea and Charbonneau left the expedition. They parted on friendly terms with Lewis and Clark and the crew.

NARRATOR 2: It's now September 23, 1806, the last day of the Lewis and Clark Expedition. Their boats are approaching the city of St. Louis. Hundreds of excited townspeople have gathered at the river to meet them. The crew fires off their rifles in salute.

TOWNSPERSON 1: Here they come! I can see their boats!

TOWNSPERSON 2: There's Captain Lewis!

NEWSPAPER REPORTER 1 (yelling a question to the crew): Did you run into fierce Indians?

CLARK: Lots of Indians, but not many fierce ones. We talked with many Indians and did some trading, and found most of them to be quite friendly.

NEWSPAPER REPORTER 2: What about wild animals?

LEWIS: I'd say we ran into the largest and fiercest carnivorous beast known to man. It stood nearly 8 feet tall, probably weighed more than 300 pounds. It's a species of bear so we called it the yellow bear. This bear had long sharp teeth and razor-sharp claws and piercing, beady eyes. It could rear up on its hind legs and let out a terrible roar. It was the biggest, meanest—

CRUZATTE: Whoa, Captain Lewis! You'll frighten the children.

LEWIS (realizing he's getting carried away): Oh! Yes, well . . . and . . . oh, we also

48

saw thousands of little barking squirrels. Very friendly animals. Harmless, totally harmless.

NEWSPAPER REPORTER 3: Did you get all the way to the Western Sea?

CLARK: Yes. But there's no way to travel directly by river. We had to go part of the way by land.

LEWIS: The new territory is much larger than we suspected, and filled with so many strange and beautiful things. We brought some samples back with us. Here, come and have a look.

(Lewis motions for the townspeople to come and see.)

NARRATOR 1: The expedition returned with a bow and arrows; Indian pottery; hundreds of samples of plant life; the skins of foxes, badgers, elk, and a yellow bear—or grizzly—skin obtained through a trade with the Sioux Indians. And, oh yes, they brought back a live "barking squirrel."

NARRATOR 2: Lewis and Clark sent Thomas Jefferson what they'd found along with a report on their journey. This information proved extremely important to the settling of the American West. Lewis and Clark's adventure opened the door for other pioneers.

Lewis and Clark
Teaching Guide

Meriwether Lewis was born in Virginia in 1774. He served in the United States Army from 1794 to 1800 and rose to the rank of captain. Lewis then went to work for Thomas Jefferson as his private secretary. He was just 29 years old when Jefferson asked him to explore the newly purchased Louisiana Territory. Lewis asked his superior officer in the Army, William Clark, to be his co-captain on the expedition. Clark, born in 1770 in Virginia, was a topographer. Their expedition lasted from May of 1804 to September of 1806. Afterwards, Lewis was named governor of the Louisiana Territory, a post he held until his death in 1809. Following Lewis's death, Clark took responsibility for publishing the journals and maps from their journey. Clark lived in St. Louis and was appointed to several government jobs including governor of the Missouri Territory and superintendent of Indian affairs, which he held until his death in 1838.

Book Links

Bold Journey: West with Lewis and Clark by Charles Bohner (Houghton Mifflin, 1985)

The Journals of Lewis and Clark abridged by Bernard De Voto (Houghton Mifflin, 1953)

Sacagawea: American Pathfinder by Flora W. Seymour (Macmillan, 1991)

EXTENSION ACTIVITIES

Talk About It

⭐ **A BARGAIN PURCHASE:** Before beginning this discussion, display a map showing the extent of the Louisiana Purchase. Ask students to locate their town or city on the map. Is it within the borders of the Louisiana Purchase? Discuss what might have happened if the United States had decided not to buy the land (which only cost us 15 million dollars!). How do students think their lives might be different today if the Louisiana Purchase had not gone through?

⭐ **ARE YOU AN EXPLORER:** Nothing was known about the vast territory contained in the Louisiana Purchase. Encourage students to imagine what it must have felt like to start on a journey into uncharted land. Would they be eager to explore, or would they just as soon someone else did it? If they had been with the Lewis and Clark expedition, what would they have been most interested in learning about: the people living in the territory, the plants, animals, birds, weather, or landscape?

Write About It

☆ **NEIGHBORHOOD JOURNALS:** Ask students to look around their own neighborhoods with the eyes of explorers. For a week, they should keep a journal recording the habits of people and plants and animals, including eating and social habits. At the end of the week, ask them to conclude their journals with paragraphs about what they learned about their neighborhood that surprised them.

☆ **NEWSPAPER ADS:** Lewis and Clark are giving a lecture! Your students are sponsoring it. Flyers must be handed out and advertisements placed in the newspaper. Ask students to design either a flyer or a newspaper ad announcing the event. Remind them to make their work as interesting and creative as possible so a large crowd will come.

Be sure to give students opportunities to share their writing via read-alouds, bulletin boards, writing walls, learning centers, and so on.

Report About It

☆ **CALLING ALL BOTANISTS:** Lewis and Clark introduced Easterners to the grizzly bear, the badger, and prairie dogs. They also collected over 150 plant samples, some of which were unfamiliar to Americans and Europeans. Let students choose an animal or plant that the expedition "discovered" and report on it. Guide those students who are interested in plants to the genera Lewisia and Clarkia, which indicate plants first found on the expedition.

☆ **EXPLORING THE SHOSHONE:** Although Sacagawea was an invaluable guide to the expedition, she is not mentioned by name in either Lewis's or Clark's journal. Lewis called her "the Indian woman" while Clark christened her Janey. Ask students to find out more about Sacagawea and the Shoshone people. How were the lives of the Shoshone affected by the westward expansion of the white settlers?

Davy Crockett
Hero of the Frontier

by Sandra Widener

Characters (in order of appearance):

NARRATOR
GENERAL ARNOLD
COLONEL ADAM ALEXANDER
DAVY CROCKETT
WOMEN 1-2
MAN 1
PRESIDENT ANDREW JACKSON

CONGRESSMEN 1-2
SOLDIERS 1-2
LIEUTENANT COLONEL
WILLIAM TRAVIS
COLONEL JIM BOWIE
SUSANNAH DICKINSON
MESSENGER

ACT 1

★★★★★ **SCENE: 1827. A campaign rally in rural Tennessee. Three candidates sit on a stage. Two are dressed in suits; the third is wearing a fringed jacket, a coonskin cap, and leather leggings. The audience is picnicking in front of the stage.**

NARRATOR: By the time Davy Crockett ran for the United States Congress, he had gained fame as a scout, a woodsman, and a bear hunter on the frontier. It was that fame—and a reputation for honesty and a shrewd wit—that led to his election to the Tennessee legislature. In 1827, Crockett's friends decided that his voice was needed in Washington.

GENERAL ARNOLD (standing and addressing the crowd): You can see, ladies and gentlemen, that he (gesturing to Adam Alexander) has no answer to my arguments! Let me tell you why Colonel Alexander, while no doubt a fine man—

WOMAN 1 (to Woman 2): He hasn't even mentioned Mr. Crockett once. It's as if he weren't even there.

WOMAN 2: General Arnold must have a reason.

GENERAL ARNOLD: Colonel Alexander had done nothing! And he will *do* nothing!

NARRATOR: The sound of a flock of guinea fowls suddenly filled the air. General Arnold's voice was drowned out, but he tried to keep talking. Finally, he was forced to stop speaking until the noise stopped. Davy Crockett stood up and faced him.

DAVY CROCKETT: Well, General, you are the first man I ever saw who understood the language of fowls. You had not the politeness even to name me in your speech. And when my little friends, the guinea hens, came up and began to holler "Crockett, Crockett, Crockett," you were ungenerous enough to drive them all away.

(The crowd breaks into laughter and applause. General Arnold looks angry and embarrassed.)

GENERAL ARNOLD: Why, I—why, why, you—you—

WOMAN 1: I'd say that Mr. Crockett answered the General in a fine fashion.

MAN 1: That old woodsman may not have spent any time in fancy clothes, but he's sharp enough for the likes of Arnold.

WOMAN 2: I confess—I think Mr. Crockett is quite a man.

MAN 1: He's got my vote! Anyone quick enough to turn a herd of guinea hens into a cheering section ought to be able to deal with our problems in Washington!

ACT 2

★★★★★ **SCENE 1: 1830. The halls of the United States Congress in Washington, D.C. As people hurry past, President Andrew Jackson and Davy Crockett are talking privately in a corner.**

NARRATOR: When the votes in the Tennessee election were counted, Davy Crockett won easily. In Washington, D.C., the new representative quickly became famous for his frontier clothes and his storytelling ability. He was also a favorite subject of newspaper stories, and people traveling to Washington fought for a view of the unlikely congressman. In 1830, Crockett faced his greatest political challenge. He opposed a popular bill that would give money to Native Americans who lived east of the Mississippi River. Crockett realized that it was an effort to force Native Americans to move west. The land they left would be snapped up by white settlers.

PRESIDENT JACKSON: If you don't support me here, you won't have a future in this congress.

DAVY CROCKETT: It's an unjust measure, and it's wicked. I'll go along with you in everything I believe right and honest. Beyond that, I will not go for any man in creation.

PRESIDENT JACKSON (becoming angry): This bill is right and honest! We'll pay the Indians!

DAVY CROCKETT: Have you *asked* the Indians what they think? I know them, and they believe this bill will destroy them.

PRESIDENT JACKSON: I'm warning you, Crockett—go against this bill, and I'll do everything in my power to defeat you when you stand for reelection. You better be prepared to give up your career.

DAVY CROCKETT: A career based on lies and dishonor is no career at all. And now, if you'll excuse me, I must say my piece about this proposed legislation.

PRESIDENT JACKSON: I'll destroy you, Crockett! I will!

SCENE 2: The House of Representatives' chamber.

NARRATOR: Davy Crockett entered the House of Representatives. When his name was called, he came forward and spoke his mind on the bill.

DAVY CROCKETT: I have always viewed the native Indian tribes of this country as a sovereign people. They have been from the time our government began. But there are those who want to juggle with the rights of the Indians and fritter them away. This is wrong! It is not justice! I would rather be an old coon dog

belonging to a poor man in the forest than belong to any party that will not do justice to all!

CONGRESSMAN 1: Who does he think he is?

CONGRESSMAN 2: Jackson will have his hide for this!

DAVY CROCKETT: The Indians are not willing to leave, and I will not consent to put them in a position where they must go. If I'm the only member of the House to vote against this bill—yes, if I'm the only man in the whole country to vote against it, I will still vote against it. It will be a matter of rejoicing to me until the day I die that I vote in the way I know is right.

CONGRESSMAN 2 (moving his head sharply to the left): Did you see that?

CONGRESSMAN 1 (looking to the left, puzzled): What?

CONGRESSMAN 2: I swear I just saw Davy Crockett's career run right out of here.

DAVY CROCKETT: I have been charged with not representing those who elected me. If that is so, the error is here (touching his head) and not here (touching his heart). I have never had wealth or education, but I have an independent spirit. When something is not right, I cannot support it. I may lose my seat here, but I will not lose my honor.

NARRATOR: President Jackson vowed to defeat Davy Crockett, and he did so in 1831. Crockett won back his seat in 1833 but, in the next election, Jackson once again fought him—and succeeded. A bitter Crockett left for Texas and a new frontier.

ACT 3
★★★★★ **SCENE 1: 1836. The Alamo, a mission built by the Spanish in Texas. It has been taken over by Texans.**

NARRATOR: Crockett landed in the town of Bexar, Texas, just in time for one of the most famous conflicts in American history—the battle of the Alamo in the war for Texas's independence from Mexico.

SOLDIER 1 (peeking through a window of the mission): Someone's coming! (taking another look) Well, I'll be. Colonel Travis, Colonel Bowie, sirs! Come take a look!

SOLDIER 2 (coming up to look, as well): That can only be one man. Those rumors were right. It's Davy Crockett himself!

DAVY CROCKETT (walking through the mission entrance dressed in buckskin and carrying his rifle): I understand you're expecting some trouble.

LIEUTENANT COLONEL WILLIAM TRAVIS (reaching out to shake Crockett's hand)**:** Welcome, sir! I'm glad to make your acquaintance, but you may not want to stay after you hear the fix we're in.

DAVY CROCKETT: I've never walked away from a tough fight, and I'm not about to start now.

COLONEL JAMES BOWIE: We've had word that the Mexican general Santa Ana is on his way with enough firepower to make things mighty uncomfortable for us.

DAVY CROCKETT: Well, I guess we'll just have to give it right back to him.

ACT 4
★★★★★★

NARRATOR: A month later, the Mexican Army led by Santa Ana had surrounded the Alamo. On guard against attack, the soldiers were scattered around the mission.

(Susannah Dickinson is taking a water bucket among the men. She stops to talk to Davy Crockett.)

DAVY CROCKETT: I don't know, Susannah. This waiting is harder than fighting. I think we had better march out and die in the open air. I don't like to be hemmed up.

SUSANNAH DICKINSON: Is there truly no hope?

DAVY CROCKETT: Not much, I'm afraid.

SUSANNAH DICKINSON: You mustn't let the boys hear you. You're the force they rally around.

(A breathless messenger runs through the gate. He runs up to Colonel Travis and salutes.)

MESSENGER: Bad news, sir! No reinforcements! And Santa Ana's on the march!

LIEUTENANT COLONEL TRAVIS: Gentlemen! Gather around! (The soldiers stand up and form a half circle around him.) You must hear the plain truth. We are 180 against thousands. Only a fool would promise victory. My resolve is clear: to remain in this mission until I die fighting. I'll draw a line in the ground (scratching a line in the dirt with his sword). Those of you who wish to leave can go and save yourselves. Those who stay must cross this line.

NARRATOR: Davy Crockett is the first to step over the line. He is followed by the other soldiers. There is a moment of silence.

LIEUTENANT COLONEL TRAVIS: All right, boys. Take your posts. For the honor of Texas!

DAVY CROCKETT: Santa Ana doesn't know what he's up against! He's about to find out what it's like to fight a man who's wrestled bears to the ground and ripped their hide off with his teeth! (raising his rifle he yells) General, take cover!

NARRATOR: Davy Crockett, along with the other 179 men in the Alamo, was killed. The women and children in the mission were spared. The war for Texas independence continued, however, and the cry "Remember the Alamo!" began to ring out during battle. Six weeks later, at the battle of San Jacinto, the Texans were victorious.

Davy Crockett
Teaching Guide

Davy Crockett was born on August 17, 1786, in Limestone, Tennessee, to poor pioneers. He had no formal education but became a skilled hunter, scout, and woodsman. He married Polly Finley in 1806 and began farming on a rented farm. In 1806, the Crocketts went in search of free land, moving near the Alabama border, where Davy became famous for his bear-hunting exploits. In 1813, after a local Indian attack, he joined General Andrew Jackson in fighting the Creek Indians. Crockett later said that this wholesale slaughter of the Creeks turned his stomach. Polly Finley Crockett died in 1815, and Crockett married Elizabeth Patton. Together, they had four children. He became a local magistrate in 1817, which meant he had to learn to read and write. Crockett then served as a colonel in the militia and for two terms, from 1821 to 1825, as a Tennessee legislator. His major aim as a congressman was to preserve the pioneers' rights to their land. It was in Washington, D.C., after his election to the House of Representatives in 1827, that Crockett gained his greatest fame. He was known as the "congressman from the canebrake." A play was written about him, and he became a celebrity based on the romantic views easterners held of the West. His principled opposition to the Indian relocation earned him President Andrew Jackson's undying enmity, however, and Crockett lost his seat in 1831. He won it in 1833, but was defeated in 1836 by Jackson's forces. Crockett left for the Texas frontier to make a new life. He died at the Alamo in 1836.

Book Links

Davy Crockett: An American Hero by Tom Townsend (Eakin Press, 1987)

Big Men, Big Country: A Collection of American Tall Tales by Paul Robert Walker (Harcourt Brace Jovanovich, 1993)

Remember the Alamo! by Robert Penn Warren (Random House, 1958)

EXTENSION ACTIVITIES

Talk About It

☆ **WHAT MAKES A HERO?:** Since his death at the Alamo, Davy Crockett has acquired the status of a folk hero in this country. Ask students which qualities they think Davy Crockett had that appealed to people so much. List them on the board.

Then ask students which other folk heroes they can name. Write the names on the board, and let students talk about why these people became so well-known and the qualities they have in common with Davy Crockett. You may wish to discuss whether different qualities appeal to people during different times. Do they think a man like Davy Crockett would be a hero today?

⭐ **FILIBUSTER, ANYONE?:** Davy Crockett was a member of the United States Congress more than 100 years ago. Talk about the ways in which Congress has changed since then. Students may mention how the area of the country has increased, as well as the population, or that gender and race no longer bar someone from running for public office. Students may also compare the issues that are in the forefront today as opposed to those of the 1830's.

Write About It

⭐ **TELLING TALL TALES:** Davy Crockett was well known for his outlandish frontier stories and witticisms. Have students write their own tall tale about Davy Crockett's frontier days. Remind them that he was known for his persuasive talking, his scouting talents, and his encounters with bears. Guide those students who wish to look up stories about Crockett and other western folk heroes for inspiration.

⭐ **LETTERS HOME:** Before the battle at the Alamo began, there was time for soldiers to write home. They knew what they faced in the coming battle. Have students imagine they are soldiers at the Alamo just after word comes that the mission will soon be under fire and they will most likely die. Ask them to write letters home from a soldier's point of view. What would they want their families to know? What would they want their last recorded words to be?

Be sure to give students opportunities to share their writing via read-alouds, bulletin boards, writing walls, learning centers, and so on.

Report About It

⭐ **EXPLORING CROCKETT'S APPEAL:** Through songs, movies, television shows, and books featuring tales about him, Davy Crockett has almost become an industry all by himself. Have students locate material from two different genres (one should be a respected biography) and compare what they learned from each. Then ask them to write essays about the differences they found, and discuss them. Which events in Davy Crockett's life were emphasized in each work, and why?

⭐ **REMEMBER THE ALAMO:** The Alamo is a well-known American battle; many students have probably heard the cry, "Remember the Alamo!" Let them research the battle and, depending upon their creative inclinations, present their findings in a variety of ways. Some may wish to write a straight-forward synopsis of the battle, while others may want to dramatize the events for radio or the stage. Other students may wish to create a replica of the mission under siege, or make a series of diagrams of the mission during the attack with captions that explain how the action unfolded.

Abraham Lincoln
Holding the Nation Together

by Meish Goldish

Characters (in order of appearance):

NARRATOR

ABRAHAM LINCOLN

NEWSPAPER REPORTERS 1-3

MARY TODD LINCOLN

OFFICER

CIVIL WAR WIDOWS 1-4

GENERAL GEORGE MEADE: A commander
of the Union Army

ACT 1

★★★★★★ SCENE: 1861. The White House. President Abraham Lincoln is answering reporters' questions.

NARRATOR: In 1861, when Abraham Lincoln took office as President of the United States, the country was sharply divided over the issue of slavery. Many Southern leaders were afraid that President Lincoln would end slavery. Eleven Southern states seceded—or withdrew—from the Union. This action led to the start of the Civil War.

REPORTER 1: Mr. Lincoln, do you intend to outlaw slavery now that you're President?

LINCOLN: I believe slavery is wrong. It goes against the ideas of democracy. I do not intend, however, to interfere with slavery in those states where the Constitution protects it.

REPORTER 2: If you don't wish to interfere, sir, then why go to war?

LINCOLN: As I've said in the past, this war is not really about slavery. It's about saving the Union. We're fighting to keep ourselves together as one nation, instead of breaking into two separate groups. I believe a house divided against itself cannot stand.

REPORTER 3: But Mr. President, nearly half of America is in favor of the United States becoming two separate nations. Why are you against it?

LINCOLN: We are a democracy. If democracy can be destroyed by a minority, then the whole idea of self-government is a failure. Suppose we do not remain one united nation. Imagine what the leaders in other countries will say. They'll say democracy doesn't work. They'll say people aren't capable of ruling themselves, that someone else must rule over them. Democracy works. We must prove that it does. To do that, we must remain united.

ACT 2

★★★★★★ SCENE: 1862. The White House. Lincoln and his wife Mary Todd Lincoln discuss the possibility of freedom for slaves.

NARRATOR: By the fall of 1862, the Civil War had expanded. Thousands of soldiers on both sides had died in battle. As the war continued, so did the fight over slavery. In the North, 200,000 black Americans served the Union as laborers, nurses, scouts, and spies. They rarely received the same amount of pay or the equipment as white people did. In the South, black people remained in slavery. Although Lincoln hadn't wanted to interfere with slavery in the Southern states, where it was legal, he was beginning to change his mind.

(Lincoln is pacing back and forth. Mary is sitting on a chair.)

MARY: Abraham, do sit down. Tell me what's on your mind.

LINCOLN *(sitting)*: I'm troubled by all the suffering I see. I see the wounded in the hospitals. I see the women who have lost husbands and sons. I see the youth of our country being cut down in their prime. And the battle continues, with no end in sight.

MARY: I know. I want my four brothers home. I don't want to think of them on a battlefield somewhere. No one wants the fighting to end more than you or I, but slavery's not about to disappear.

LINCOLN: That's why I must change my tactics now.

MARY: What do you mean?

LINCOLN: It means the slaves must be set free. Slavery must finally be outlawed in the South. It's the only way to reunite the country.

MARY: Tolerating slavery where it already exists is one thing. Outlawing it is another. It will make you even more unpopular in the South than you already are.

LINCOLN: Mary, listen to me. The Declaration of Independence promised freedom and equality for all Americans—all Americans. Right now, negroes don't enjoy that equality. They're not allowed to be citizens. That's wrong, Mary. It's wrong.

MARY: I worry enough as it is about your safety. Do you realize what a dangerous step this is for you to take?

LINCOLN: I know it's dangerous, Mary, but I cannot be a strong leader if I'm a coward in my personal convictions.

ACT 3
★★★★★★ **SCENE: 1862. Lincoln is at his desk in the Oval Office.**

(An officer knocks and then enters the office.)

OFFICER: Excuse me, Mister President, but a group of war widows asks if you might see them now.

LINCOLN: Yes, of course. Send them in.

(Four women enter the room.)

LINCOLN: Please, ladies, sit down. *(They all sit.)* I am very sorry for your losses.

WIDOW 1: Nothing can be done to bring them back. We do beg you, please, Mr.

President, to call an end to the fighting immediately, so no one else has to suffer as we do.

LINCOLN: My heart goes out to you, and to all the other widows and mothers who suffer.

WIDOW 2: Then why can't you simply declare an end to the conflict?

LINCOLN: You have suffered terrible losses. I ask you to consider what the slaves in the South are suffering. They are living without freedom, without rights. Their suffering has lasted for generations. As long as slavery remains legal, they will continue to suffer for generations more. That is not democracy.

WIDOW 3: But why did my husband have to die for that?

WIDOW 4: The war has lasted for over a year. How many more men must die? You must do something, sir!

LINCOLN: I intend to. I don't know that it is what you wish me to do, but it must be done. I now feel that this war will not end until slavery is abolished entirely. The slaves must be emancipated.

NARRATOR: Abraham Lincoln was true to his word. On January 1, 1863, he issued the Emancipation Proclamation. It stated that slaves in states rebelling against the Union were now free. Unfortunately, Lincoln's declaration did not end the Civil War. The Southern states ignored the order, and the fighting continued. The Proclamation, however, did send a signal to all Americans that the country was headed in a new direction.

ACT 4
★★★★★ SCENE: November 19, 1863. Gettysburg, Pennsylvania.
Lincoln and General Meade are sitting on an outdoor stage. Meade is at the podium.

NARRATOR: In July, 1863, the Union army, led by General George Meade, won a large and important battle at Gettysburg, Pennsylvania. More than 40,000 soldiers were killed and wounded in the fighting. A few months later, it was decided that part of the battlefield would be set aside as a cemetery for those who died there. Lincoln attended the dedication ceremony to deliver perhaps his most famous speech ever—the Gettysburg Address.

GENERAL MEADE: Ladies and gentlemen, the President of the United States.

(There is applause.)

LINCOLN: *Fourscore and seven years ago, our fathers brought forth on this continent a new nation, conceived in liberty, and dedicated to the proposition that all men are created* *equal. Now we are engaged in a great civil war, testing whether that nation, or any nation so conceived and so dedicated, can long endure. We are met on a great battlefield of that war. We have come to dedicate a portion of that field as a final resting-place for those who here gave their lives that that nation might live. It is altogether fitting and proper that we should do this. But, in a larger sense, we cannot dedicate—we cannot consecrate—we cannot hallow this ground. The brave men, living and dead, who struggled here, have consecrated it far above our poor power to add or detract. The world will little note, nor long remember what we say here, but it can never forget what they did here. It is for us the living, rather to be dedicated here to the unfinished work which they, who fought here have thus far so nobly advanced. It is rather for us to be here dedicated to the great task remaining before us—that from these honored dead we take increased devotion to that cause for which they gave the last full measure of devotion; that we here highly resolve that these dead shall not have died in vain; that this nation, under God, shall have a new birth of freedom, and that government of the people, by the people, for the people, shall not perish from the earth.*

NARRATOR: Lincoln's speech lasted only three minutes. Some people say that the Gettysburg Address helped turn the tide of the Civil War. For although the fighting continued for another year and a half, Lincoln's words gave the Union the inspiration that it needed to finally achieve victory. As Mary Lincoln had feared, her husband's life did end in tragedy. Lincoln's dreams did not die with him. The Emancipation Proclamation was the start of a long struggle for civil rights and equality for all Americans.

Abraham Lincoln
Teaching Guide

Abraham Lincoln was born in a log cabin in Harden, Kentucky, on February 12, 1809. The Lincolns eventually moved to Indiana, and young Abraham grew up on the frontier. Although he had less than a year of formal schooling, Lincoln was known to walk several miles to obtain books to read. In 1831, he moved on his own to New Salem, Illinois, where he worked as a store clerk and later as the town's postmaster. Lincoln won election to the state legislature in 1834; he quickly became known as a skilled and witty debater. He went on to receive a law license and practice law in Illinois. In 1842, Lincoln married Mary Todd. They had four sons, three of whom led relatively short lives due to illnesses. Lincoln ran on the Republican ticket for president in 1860 and was victorious. Re-elected as president in 1864, he saw the Civil War end the following year. His personal triumph was short lived. Five days after the South's surrender to the North, he was assassinated by John Wilkes Booth. Lincoln died on April 15, 1865.

Book Links

Lincoln's Birthday by Dennis Brindell Fradin (Enslow, 1990)

Lincoln: A Photobiography by Russell Freedman (Clarion, 1987)

Abraham Lincoln by Jim Hargrove (Children's Press, 1988)

Abraham Lincoln: To Preserve the Union by Russell Shorto (Silver Burdett, 1990)

EXTENSION ACTIVITIES

Talk About It

☆ **LINCOLN LEGACIES:** Ask students to come up with a list of ways that Abraham Lincoln is remembered and honored by Americans today. Write their responses on the board. Students might mention Lincoln's likeness on the penny and the five-dollar bill; observance of his birthday (on Presidents' Day); the Lincoln Memorial; his likeness on Mount Rushmore; and towns, schools, and institutions named after him. Ask students why they think Lincoln is commemorated in so many ways. What do they believe were his greatest contributions to the country? What, if any, do they feel were his weaknesses?

☆ **CIVIL WAR CONVERSATIONS:** Organize students into cooperative groups of four or five. Let them discuss these questions: Why do you think Lincoln chose at first not to interfere with slavery in the southern states? Do you think it was right or wise for him to change his mind later? How might the course of the nation have been different without the Emancipation Proclamation? Have each group predict events that might have occurred had there been no Proclamation and list them on paper. Invite each group to share its list aloud. Allow time for groups to comment on each other's lists.

Write About It

☆ **LINCOLN PLAQUES:** Lincoln is one of America's most revered presidents. Ask students to create a special plaque in honor of him. The plaque should contain a list of reasons why Lincoln deserves to be honored. Students may make the plaque out of cardboard, construction paper, or other available materials.

☆ **POLITICAL CARTOONS:** Political cartoonists often emphasize one physical characteristic of a person in their drawings. After giving students the opportunity to study a variety of current political cartoons, provide them with several photographs of Lincoln and ask them to draw their own political cartoons featuring Lincoln. They should set their cartoons in the 1860s. If students are insecure about their artistic abilities, stress that the aim is not draw an exact likeness of Lincoln but rather a figure that suggests him.

Be sure to give students opportunities to share their writing via read-alouds, bulletin boards, writing walls, learning centers, and so on.

Report About It

☆ **WARTIME JOUNALISTS:** Some residents of Washington, D.C., rode on horseback and in carriages to Bull Run in northern Virginia to watch the first battle of the Civil War. Ask students to imagine they were newspaper reporters during the Civil War. After they have researched an important battle of the war, such as Antietam, Bull Run, Gettysburg, Shiloh, or Vicksburg, have them write a news account of the battle, indicating the importance of the outcome.

☆ **TORN LOYALTIES:** Not all Northerners were abolitionists and not all Southerners favored secession. Not only was the Union itself divided, but many families were divided in their sympathies. Discuss students' perceptions of Northerners and Southerners before and during the Civil War. Then ask them to do research on a person from either side who goes against those perceptions.

☆ **EXPLORE CIVIL RIGHTS:** The Emancipation Proclamation was a beginning step in the fight for civil rights. Invite pairs of students to find out more about another important civil rights leader of the past or present, such as Harriet Tubman or Reverend Jesse Jackson. Then challenge each pair of students to compare and contrast the life and character of Lincoln with that of the individual. Encourage partners to share their reports with the class.

Susan B. Anthony
The Fight for Women's Rights

by Helen H. Moore

Characters (in order of appearance):

NARRATORS 1-2

SUSAN B. ANTHONY: A feminist (a person who works for equality between men and women)

GUELMA ANTHONY:
HANNAH ANTHONY: } Susan's sisters
MARY ANTHONY:

ELIZABETH CADY STANTON: A feminist and a friend of Susan's

JUSTICE WARD HUNT

MR. HENRY SELDEN: A lawyer and friend of Susan's

JURY OF 12 MEN

SPECTATOR 1

SPECTATORS 2-8 (nonspeaking roles)

ACT 1

★★★★★ **SCENE:** 1872. The front hallway of Susan B. Anthony's house in New York, 1872. Susan, her three sisters, and her friend Elizabeth Cady Stanton are about to leave for the polling place.

NARRATOR 1: In the early 1800s, American women, like enslaved African and Native Americans, were not allowed to vote. Most women did not receive much education, or work at jobs outside the home. If a woman did work, and she was married, her husband had the legal right to take all the money she earned. If her parents died, and left their money to her, all of it automatically became her husband's property—not hers. If he lost all his own money, through gambling or bad investments, he had the right to sell all of his wife's belongings—even her clothing—to pay off his debt! And although divorces were rare, if a woman did get divorced, the custody of her children would automatically go to her husband. That was the law.

NARRATOR 2: Not everyone believed the laws were fair. Susan B. Anthony was one American who thought the laws should be changed. The greatest law of the land was (and is) the United States Constitution. Any law—even the Constitution—can be changed, if enough people vote to change it. Susan and the other feminists knew that women had to get the right to vote first before the laws could be changed and women gained equal rights.

HANNAH: I'm so nervous! We could go to jail for this!

SUSAN: People only go to jail for breaking the law.

GUELMA: It's against the law for us to vote, isn't it?

MARY: I'm confused. The Constitution doesn't say *anything* about women having the right to vote.

SUSAN: That's right. It doesn't say we have the right—but it doesn't say we don't.

GUELMA: Well, make up your mind. Do we or don't we? Which is it?

SUSAN: I've done a lot of thinking about this. The Constitution states that all people born in the United States are citizens . . .

GUELMA: Right.

SUSAN: and that the states shall make no law that denies any person the rights of citizenship . . .

HANNAH, GUELMA, AND MARY: So . . . ?

SUSAN: So, if we are persons . . .

HANNAH, GUELMA, AND MARY: (looking at each other and nodding) Which we are!

SUSAN: born in the United States . . .

HANNAH, GUELMA, AND MARY: Which we were!

SUSAN: then we're citizens. And one of the "rights of citizenship" is the right to vote. No state can deny us that right.

HANNAH: We-e-e-l-l-l-l, when you put it that way, I guess we do have the right. But if we already have the right, why is it that women don't vote?

SUSAN: A few women have. They're allowed to fill out a ballot, but as soon as they leave the polling place, their ballots are thrown away. They're not counted. And many women, sad to say, don't yet realize how important voting is.

ELIZABETH: That's right! They're content to let their husbands "support" and "protect" them!

MARY: But what about women who aren't married?

GUELMA: Or women who have bad husbands?

HANNAH: What are they to do?

ELIZABETH: Society calls them old maids and expects them to go and live with relatives. If they have no relatives, they wind up in the poor house, or on the streets, because they have no education and no way to support themselves.

HANNAH: It's so sad.

SUSAN: It is, and it will be, until we women can help change our country's laws.

MARY: Well, what are we waiting for? Let's go vote!

ACT 2

★★★★★ **SCENE: A courtroom in a tiny village in New York State. Susan and her lawyer Henry Selden sit at the defense table. Elizabeth Cady Stanton and Susan's sisters are among the spectators. In addition to a judge, there is a jury of 12 men.**

NARRATOR 1: Susan and her sisters had decided to cast votes in the 1872 presidential election to test Susan's theory. The voting inspectors *did* allow them to cast their ballots, but . . .

NARRATOR 2: Two weeks after the election Susan was arrested and charged with voter fraud—a very serious offense. She was tried by Justice Ward Hunt in front of a jury of 12 men.

SUSAN: Your honor, I wish to ask permission to act as my own lawyer—

JUDGE HUNT (banging his gavel): Permission denied! Be seated!

SUSAN (returning to her seat and whispering to her attorney)**:** Well, Henry, it's up to you.

HENRY: Don't worry, Susan. I know your reasons for voting. When I explain them to the judge and the jury, they'll understand, too.

SUSAN: I hope so!

(As Henry rises and approaches the bench, Susan leans back to whisper to Elizabeth. She nods at the all-male jury and the male judge.)

SUSAN: It's a man's world in here, that's for sure! Is it possible for any woman to get justice?

ELIZABETH: Henry is a good man, and a good lawyer. He'll do his best to see justice done.

HENRY: Your honor, my client is a patriotic American. She is hard-working, and she pays her taxes. She has studied the law, and she believes that the Constitution gives her, as a citizen, the right to vote.

HUNT (snickering)**:** Your client has studied the law, you say? If your client had stuck to her womanly duties, instead of trying to understand things like the law, which are beyond women, she wouldn't be in my courtroom today!

HENRY: I object, your honor! Susan B. Anthony is no criminal! If she were a man, we'd *praise* her for voting! She wants to do her duty for her country, just as you and I do. She believes the Constitution gives her and all women the right to vote—

HUNT: Do her duty for her country as you and I do? Hah! That's a good one. What's next? Will these women be wanting to serve in the army, like men? (The male spectators and jurors laugh.) Stand back, Mr. Selden. I'm ready to give my verdict.

HENRY: Your honor!

NARRATOR 1: The jury foreman looks surprised. He holds up a finger as if he's about to speak, but the judge silences him with a glance, and a bang of the gavel.

NARRATOR 2: The spectators whisper among themselves. Even the people who don't agree with Susan B. Anthony's fight realize that what the judge is doing is wrong.

HUNT: Susan B. Anthony, approach the bench.

NARRATOR 1: She does. The judge takes a piece of paper, which he has had in his pocket through the whole trial, and reads from it.

HUNT (reading from the piece of paper)**:** I find you guilty of voting fraudulently!

NARRATOR 2: Susan and her supporters are shocked. They look at the jury, but the members are looking at each other in confusion.

ELIZABETH: The judge made up his mind in advance! This trial was dishonest!

SUSAN: Your honor, shouldn't the jury decide?

HUNT: You're out of order! This is *my* courtroom, and I make the rules. You're guilty as charged. I fine you the sum of $100.

HENRY: Your honor!

SUSAN (furiously): Judge Hunt, I will not pay one cent of this unjust fine!

SPECTATOR: I guess this will put an end to all your talk of voting like a man!

SUSAN (turning to face him): An end? Not at all. I'll never stop working until all American women have the right to vote!

NARRATOR 1: As she promised, Susan B. Anthony never paid her fine. She could have been put in prison for her refusal to pay. Judge Hunt knew, however, that if Susan were imprisoned, she could have appealed his decision to a higher court. That court might have punished the judge for unethical conduct because he decided the verdict himself—in advance—without listening to the jury.

NARRATOR 2: Until her death at the age of 86, Susan B. Anthony continued to lead the fight for women's suffrage. In 1920, 14 years after her death and exactly 100 years after her birth, Congress passed the Susan B. Anthony Amendment to the Constitution which gave all American women the right to vote at last!

Susan B. Anthony
Teaching Guide

Susan Brownell Anthony was born on February 15, 1820, in Adams, Massachusetts. Her father was a well-to-do Quaker, a progressive though spiritual man who encouraged all his children, daughters as well as sons, to think for themselves and to work for social justice. Susan's mother was not a Quaker, but she respected her husband's Quaker values of equality and temperance. To advance the cause of women's suffrage, Susan B. Anthony became a popular public speaker, writer, and newspaper publisher of *The Revolution*. She voted in 1872 in order to test the theory that women already had the constitutional right to vote. When denied in this effort, she and other feminists concentrated on having a women's suffrage amendment added to the Constitution. This effort finally succeeded in 1920 with the ratification of the 19th or the "Susan B. Anthony" Amendment, which states that "the right of citizens of the United States to vote shall not be denied or abridged by the United States or any state on account of sex."

Book Links

Susan B. Anthony: A Crusade for Womanhood by Gwendolyn J. Crenshaw and the AESOP Enterprises, Inc. Staff (AESOP, 1991)

Susan B. Anthony by Ilene Cooper (Franklin Watts, NY, 1984)

Susan B. Anthony: Champion of Women's Rights by Helen A. Monsell (Macmillan, 1986)

EXTENSION ACTIVITIES

Talk About It

☆ **CAREER SURVEY:** Some things have changed a great deal since Anthony's day; others have not. Discuss some of the changes in women's and men's roles, and then take a survey: ask students about their career plans. Are there any girls who plan to be doctors, or lawyers, or plumbers? Do any boys plan to be nurses or teachers? Write the girls' career choices in one column on the board, and the boys' in another. Talk about the results: Does your survey indicate that while girls are leaning toward what were once "male" careers, boys are not considering traditionally "female" jobs? Are some boys interested in becoming nurses and teachers but reluctant to admit it?

Do some girls want to work in the home but are reluctant also to mention it? What do students think the results mean about their own attitudes toward men's and women's roles?

⭐ **MEDIA WATCH:** Susan B. Anthony challenged the law to make a point. She knew that her interpretation of the Constitution was not likely to be upheld. She bent the law in order to demonstrate the need for change. Ask students to scan newspapers and watch the national news for examples of modern-day activists who challenge laws they feel are wrong. Discuss whether there are instances where people must bend the law, as Anthony did, in order to change it. Do they have the right to do so? If they do, what gives them the right? If not, why not? What would students have done in Anthony's day? As an extension, students may be interested in researching the United States Constitution and the Bill of Rights.

Write About It

⭐ **CLASS PETITIONS:** Susan B. Anthony changed history by working to change the law. Invite groups of students to work cooperatively to identify issues they may want to change. Once each group has identified an issue, the class can vote on one issue to work on as a whole group. Have students work collaboratively to draft a petition, collect signatures, and/or write a letter to elected officials and local newspapers in your area to effect change.

⭐ **EDITORIAL DUETS:** Despite her stances on issues such as abolition, temperance, and women's suffrage, Susan B. Anthony was admired and respected by many people who held opposite views. Her newspaper, *The Revolution*, provided a forum for Anthony to express her opinions. Divide the class into pairs. Give one partner in each pair a pro or con stance on women's suffrage, and then have him or her write an editorial supporting that position. The other partner should read the editorial and then write a rebuttal. You may wish to bring in newspaper Op Ed pages to allow students to become familiar with editorials.

Be sure to give students opportunities to share their writing via read-alouds, bulletin boards, writing walls, learning centers, and so on.

Report About It

⭐ **REBELS WITH A CAUSE:** In her day, Susan B. Anthony was one of many people working for social change. Encourage students to report on another activist who has influenced American life. You may wish to suggest Elizabeth Cady Stanton, Lucretia Mott, Frederick Douglass, Sojourner Truth, Rosa Parks, or Amelia Bloomer.

⭐ **ERA EXPERTS:** Invite students to research the ERA (Equal Rights Amendment). What is it? Why do its supporters believe the amendment is needed? Have any states adopted equal rights amendments? Why hasn't a national amendment been passed yet? What do students think about the ERA?

Harriet Tubman
Guide to Freedom

by Susan Moger

Characters (in order of appearance):

NARRATORS 1-2

GROUP ESCAPING FROM
   SLAVERY

JOHNNY: An eight-year-old boy

MOTHER: Johnny and Sally's
   mother

SALLY: A ten-year-old girl

THOMAS

FRANK

HARRIET TUBMAN

OVERSEER

JIM: A slave trying to escape

MINTY: Harriet Tubman at
   the age of thirteen

RIT: Harriet's mother

MEN 1-2

BOY

PASSENGERS 1-6
   (nonspeaking roles)

WILLIAM STILL: A Black
   member of the Vigilance
   Committee in Philadelphia

PROLOGUE
★ ★ ★ ★ ★ ★ ★ ★ SCENE: The 1850s. The Maryland woods. Two men and a mother with two children wait in a clearing. It is early evening on a cold December night. The group stays close together and pays attention to every sound.

NARRATOR 1: In 1849 Harriet Tubman escaped from slavery in Maryland and went to Philadelphia where she could live as a free person. Along the way, she was helped by people—white and black—on the Underground Railroad. Harriet Tubman did not stay in the North where she was safe. During the 1850s, she made 19 carefully planned trips back to Maryland to guide hundreds of people out of slavery. Since Sunday was a day of rest for slaves, Harriet would meet groups of runaways on Saturday nights so they could get a day's head start before they were missed. Sometimes she met the groups on holidays when their owners were busy with parties and dinners.

NARRATOR 2: These five people have gathered in the woods because they received a coded message that Harriet, known as Moses, would meet them here. They've been waiting in the clearing for six hours.

JOHNNY: Mama, I'm so cold I can't stand it.

MOTHER: Hush, now. If Moses says she'll be here, she'll be here, Johnny.

SALLY: Why is she called Moses anyway, Mama? That's a man's name!

THOMAS: Shh. Shh! What's that—an owl?

FRANK: Owl or dog. Coming this way.

MOTHER: You there! Frank! Don't you scare my children! (turning to Sally) She's called Moses because in the Bible Moses led his people out of slavery in Egypt to the promised land. And that's just what this Moses does, too. She's going to lead us all out to freedom.

JOHNNY: Freedom? Where's that? I thought we were going to Canada!

THOMAS: Moses is just about braver than any man I know.

FRANK: They say she'll shoot you if you try to turn back. "Nobody goes back." That's her motto.

MOTHER: Do you believe *everything* you hear, Frank?

FRANK: I heard she has spells, too—just falls asleep without even knowing it.

THOMAS: Now that's true. She was hit in the head by a no-good overseer when she was a little bitty thing. He was a hard, hard man. She's never been the same since. She got away in the end, though. Yes sir, all the way to Philadelphia.

SALLY: But she's come back for us. I'm glad about that.

JOHNNY: I hope she comes soon. I sure am cold.

SALLY: Tell us more about Moses. Please?

ACT 1

★★★★★ **SCENE: 1834. The general store at a crossroads near the Brodas Plantation in Maryland.**

NARRATOR 1: Harriet Tubman was born into slavery in about 1821. Her parents, Ben and Rit, called her Minty. Minty, her parents, and her nine brothers and sisters were slaves. They "belonged" to a plantation owner named Brodas. As slaves, they owned nothing and were paid nothing for their work. Their time, their energy, and their lives belonged to Brodas. At any time, husbands, wives, and children could be sold and taken away to work for different masters. It happened to Minty's family. Her two older sisters were sold when they were very young. Ben and Rit couldn't do anything about it.

NARRATOR 2: Minty never forgot seeing her sisters taken away. They were crying, and ropes were tied around their ankles. As she grew older, she heard whispered stories about people who escaped and traveled north—to freedom. When Minty was 13 years old, she had her first chance to help someone escape. Jim was the first of many whom Harriet Tubman helped.

NARRATOR 1: Jim runs into the general store and hides under the counter. The plantation overseer follows Jim, and Minty follows the overseer. She stops in the doorway.

OVERSEER (to Jim): Get out from under that counter! I'll whip you good when I get my hands on you. Where do you think you're going anyway?

JIM: Leave me alone! I ain't hurting nobody!

MINTY: Jim!

OVERSEER: Stay out of here, girl. I've got to tie him up.

MINTY: NO! Jim, run! Now!

OVERSEER: He's getting away! You little—!

NARRATOR 2: Minty steps away from the door. Jim runs out of the store. The overseer is so angry he picks up a heavy weight from the store's scale and throws it after Jim. It hits Minty in the center of her forehead. She falls to the floor. Her mother Rit comes running into the store.

RIT: Minty, oh Minty! You've killed her!

76

OVERSEER: You there, you just stand back. She's only faking.

NARRATOR 1: Harriet Tubman was badly hurt. She eventually recovered, but for the rest of her life she suffered headaches and sudden attacks of sleepiness. The incident left her with a huge scar on her head—and a relentless desire for freedom in her heart. After this, people called her Harriet, not Minty, out of respect for her courage in helping Jim.

ACT 2
★★★★★★ SCENE: The 1850s. A railroad station in Maryland. Two men are talking. One of them hangs up a poster promising a reward for Harriet Tubman's capture. Several people, including a young boy and an old woman holding a book, are waiting for a train.

NARRATOR 1: Harriet escaped from Maryland in 1849. Her husband John Tubman, already a free man, refused to go with her because he didn't want to leave Maryland. Harriet had no choice but to go without him. She made her way to Philadelphia, helped along the way by the Underground Railroad. This wasn't a railroad with trains and tracks, but a network of people who provided transportation and shelter to those escaping from slavery. Harriet didn't stay in Philadelphia for long.

NARRATOR 2: In 1850, Congress passed the Fugitive Slave Law. It allowed slave hunters to capture former slaves anywhere in the United States and return them to the South. Rather than moving to Canada where she would have been safe, Harriet Tubman returned to Maryland to help others escape. Sometimes she brought people north in carriages, sometimes they walked, sometimes they rode the real trains; but whatever the mode of transportation, the "station masters" and "conductors" of the Underground Railroad were always behind the plan. They made sure coded messages got through, and helped the escaping slaves move safely from place to place, all the way to the Canadian border.

NARRATOR 1: News of Harriet Tubman's rescues spread. Slave owners wanted her trips stopped because they believed she was stealing their property. The owners hired slave hunters and posted signs offering rewards for Harriet's capture—dead or alive. The threat of death didn't stop her. She bravely carried out her mission under the very noses of those hunting her.

MAN 1: See this poster? It says here there's a $10,000 reward.

MAN 2: "Short; middle-aged woman; unable to read or write; carries a pistol." I've heard of her. They call her Moses, don't they? Somebody over in Baltimore seen her. Said she was six feet tall and dressed as a man.

MAN 1: Man or woman, she's got a bad scar on her head that she can't hide.

MAN 2: Well, ain't nobody around here but that old woman and that little boy. You want me to check 'em? I guess if she can make herself grow into a big old man, she can turn herself into a little boy just as easy.

MAN 1: Shut up and hang up some of these posters. We've got to stop her stealing people's lawful property.

NARRATOR 1: The two men move on. Out of the corner of her eye, the old woman watches them disappear. When she's sure the men have gone, she puts down her book. It's Harriet Tubman!

HARRIET (to herself): Well, it worked. I guess I was holding this book the right way up! (aloud) Boy! Psst! Boy!

BOY: Yes, ma'am?

HARRIET: Come on over here. I'll pay you five pennies to go along behind those men and tear down those posters. Now, don't let them see you. Can you do that?

BOY: Yes, ma'am! I won't let them see me. Aren't you—

HARRIET: Thank you kindly for your help. And here's another penny for a promise: You can't say a word about any of this.

ACT 3
★★★★★ **SCENE: A few months later. The home of William Still, a "conductor" on the Underground Railroad. Harriet and William are talking.**

WILLIAM: Harriet, it's way too dangerous for you to go back to Maryland. You're too well known. The reward's up to $10,000.

HARRIET: I know; I've seen the posters. But I have to go. They're expecting me.

WILLIAM: Can't you at least wait a while?

HARRIET: No. They've been waiting long enough as it is. They whispered to me as I passed by six months ago. I sent a message that I'd come back at Christmas. We're meeting in the woods near the crossroads. I have to be there.

WILLIAM: It's too dangerous! The slave hunters are all over Maryland now. And with that scar of yours—

HARRIET: I can hide my scar, but I can't ask my people to bear the scars of slavery one more day.

WILLIAM: Please be careful.

HARRIET: Oh, William, I thank you for your concern. I haven't lost anyone yet, and I don't intend to.

EPILOGUE

★ ★ ★ ★ ★ ★ ★ ★ ★ **SCENE:** The clearing in the Maryland woods. It is an hour later. Johnny and Sally, their mother, Thomas, and Frank continue to wait for Harriet Tubman in the clearing in the Maryland woods.

JOHNNY: But how can Moses tell us which way to go? It's so dark. We could go south instead of north.

(*Harriet steps out from behind a tree.*)

HARRIET: Good evening.

JOHNNY AND SALLY: Moses!

HARRIET: I'll show you how to find your way in the dark. Look up there. See that bright star? That's the North Star. We'll be following it till sunrise. And when the stars are hidden by clouds, we'll feel the trees.

SALLY: Feel the trees?

HARRIET: Moss grows on the north side of trees. If you feel moss, you know that tree's facing north.

JOHNNY: North to freedom!

HARRIET: To freedom. We'd better get started. We have a long way to go.

Harriet Tubman
Teaching Guide

After her own escape from slavery in 1849, Harriet Tubman helped over 300 people to freedom. On her first return trip to the South, Harriet brought out her sister; in 1854, her three brothers; and, in 1857, her parents. During the Civil War, she volunteered as a nurse, a scout, and a spy for the Union Army. Working behind enemy lines in South Carolina, Harriet guided many more slaves to freedom. When the Civil War ended, she settled in Auburn, New York, with her parents and brothers. In 1869 her biography, *Scenes in the Life of Harriet Tubman*, was written by Sarah Bradford, a white woman who donated all the proceeds of the book to Harriet. The Tubman home in Auburn had become a haven for the elderly and sick, and Harriet continually needed money to care for them. In 1886 Sarah Bradford published a second biography, *Harriet Tubman, the Moses of Her People*. During these years, Harriet also gave lectures and joined with Elizabeth Cady Stanton and Susan B. Anthony in fighting for women's rights. Harriet Tubman died in 1913 at the age of 92. She was given a full military funeral and was honored by the city of Auburn with a bronze plaque in front of the courthouse. It cites her "rare courage" as "the Moses of her people."

Book Links

Go Free or Die: A Story About Harriet Tubman by Jeri Ferris (Carolrhoda Books, 1988)

The Story of Harriet Tubman by Kate McMullan (Dell Yearling, 1991)

Freedom Train: The Story of Harriet Tubman by Dorothy Sterling (Scholastic, 1987)

EXTENSION ACTIVITIES

Talk About It

⭐ **WHAT WOULD YOU DO?:** A $10,000 price was put on Harriet Tubman's head. In the 1850s that was a considerable amount of money—much more than $10,000 means to us today. Ask students to think about how they would feel if it were their faces on the posters. Would they stop helping people? Do they feel Harriet Tubman was a courageous person? Who else do they consider to be courageous? Bring up the fact that not all courageous acts are big acts that affect a lot of people. Ask students to share times when they had to act courageously.

☆ **THE POWER OF THE BOOK:** If possible, bring in Frederick Douglass's autobiography. Read to the class the section where Douglass tells how he taught himself to read and write. Then open a discussion about why the slave owners didn't want their workers to have an education. To spur ideas, ask questions such as: Couldn't the owners get even more work out of people if they were educated? Couldn't they take over more jobs?

Write About It

☆ **CODED MESSAGES:** Harriet Tubman could neither read nor write. As discussed above, many enslaved people were denied education. What form did the coded messages take that detailed the meeting times and places with members of the Underground Railroad? Let students compose their own coded messages without using written words. They may devise a spoken code or use pictures and drawings to create a written one.

☆ **EXPLORING TUBMAN'S INFLUENCE:** Sometimes one person can have a great impact on another person's life. Harriet Tubman directly helped changed hundreds of lives. Indirectly, her actions affected a wide array of people from plantation owners in the last century to civil rights activists in this century. After students have read or enacted the play, ask them to choose one of the characters in the play who interacted with Harriet Tubman. Encourage them to think about how that character might have changed because of Harriet Tubman, and then have them write about it.

Be sure to give students opportunities to share their writing via read-alouds, bulletin boards, writing walls, learning centers, and so on.

Report About It

☆ **MAPPING THE ESCAPE ROUTES:** Like a real railway system, the Underground Railroad had different routes. Have students trace the most famous Underground Railroad routes on a map and calculate the distances escaping slaves had to travel from Maryland to freedom before and after 1850 when the Fugitive Slave Act was passed. Ask them to report their findings in a written report or in a graph. Encourage students to be creative in their approaches; they may incorporate art into their graphs or they may choose to write a poem or song.

☆ **CIVIL RIGHTS TIMELINE:** The end of the Civil War meant the legal end of slavery. In what ways were African Americans still denied full citizenship and equality? Guide students in researching legislation and court cases that have directly affected African Americans. You may wish to expand the search from the 1600's to the present day. After everyone has presented her or his report, suggest the class make a time line recording these events.

John Muir
The Father of National Parks

by Frank Caropreso

Characters (in order of appearance):

NARRATOR

JOHN MUIR: Naturalist

LOUIE MUIR: Wife of John Muir

HELEN MUIR: Daughter of John and Louie Muir

WANDA MUIR: Daughter of John and Louie Muir

THEODORE ROOSEVELT: 26th President of United States

ARCHIE LEONARD: Ranger, mountaineer, and guide

CHARLES LIEDIG: Ranger, cook, and guide

NEWSPAPER REPORTER

PARKS COMMISSIONERS 1-4

GEORGE C. PARDEE: Governor of California

ACT 1

★★★★★★ SCENE: Spring 1903. The Muir house in California. John Muir, his wife Louie, and their daughters Helen and Wanda are sitting on the front porch. A special delivery letter has just been delivered to John Muir.

NARRATOR: In 1903, the United States was growing as an industrial nation. The country's natural resources were being abused by some land developers, timber companies, and ranchers. A handful of naturalists saw how important it was to protect nature and to keep it safe for future generations. John Muir was one of those naturalists. On a camping trip in Yosemite Valley, he convinced President Theodore Roosevelt that land should be set aside in national parks. John Muir almost didn't go on that camping trip with Roosevelt . . .

LOUIE: Who's the letter from, John?

MUIR (reading a letter and shaking his head)**:** I don't see how I can do it.

HELEN: Do what, Daddy?

MUIR: I've been planning this trip to Japan and China and Russia for so long . . . I don't see how I can drop that to go to Yosemite.

WANDA: Who wants you to go to Yosemite?

MUIR: I'm sorry, Wanda. Did you say something?

WANDA: Who wants you to go to Yosemite, Dad?

MUIR: The President. Teddy Roosevelt himself. Listen to this: "I want to drop politics for four days and be in the open with you."

WANDA: That's great!

HELEN: Can we all go?

MUIR: I don't see how. The dates the President wants to go camping would mean delaying my trip.

LOUIE: John, you have to go with the President. It's an honor.

WANDA: And besides, once you've got him in Yosemite, he'll listen to you. He'll see for himself how much it needs to be protected.

MUIR: I had my heart set on seeing those trees in Asia—

LOUIE: And they'll be there next year. You need to concentrate on the trees in Yosemite. If Roosevelt listens to the wrong people, you may have to go to Asia to see any trees at all.

HELEN: Daddy—if I can't go to Yosemite, can I go to Japan in your place?

ACT 2

★★★★★ **SCENE:** A hotel in Yosemite valley. Four parks commissioners are waiting for Roosevelt to arrive.

NARRATOR: The Parks Commission was a group of state officials who were supposed to look after Yosemite valley. Some of the commissioners were more interested in making Yosemite a money-making attraction. Under their care, more roads and buildings appeared in the valley. John Muir's belief that Yosemite should be under the control of the federal government didn't sit well with those commissioners.

COMMISSIONER 1: We have a real good chance to get Roosevelt to see things our way on this trip.

COMMISSIONER 2: Listen, after all the parties and the food and a good night's rest on the softest bed in this hotel, he'll pay attention to us, I guarantee it.

COMMISSIONER 3: Wait till he sees the valley all lit up by the floodlights! I mean it. Is there a prettier sight?

COMMISSIONER 4: Pretty soon Teddy will forget all about taking Yosemite out of our hands.

COMMISSIONER 1: But what about Muir?

COMMISSIONER 2: Don't worry about him. I've made sure his room is nowhere near Roosevelt's—

COMMISSIONER 3: Ssh! Ssh! Here comes the President now.

NARRATOR: Teddy Roosevelt came to Yosemite prepared to camp out. Muir was with him as well as Archie Leonard, who was a ranger, a mountaineer and a guide; and Charles Liedig, who was a ranger, a cook, and a guide. Roosevelt hadn't come to Yosemite for parties and light shows.

COMMISSIONERS 1, 2, 3: Welcome to Yosemite, Mr. President!

COMMISSIONER 2: Oh, and you, too, Muir.

ROOSEVELT: Thank you, gentlemen. It's a bully place.

COMMISSIONER 1: Welcome, welcome. Your luggage is at the hotel, sir. And we have a big party planned for you later—

ROOSEVELT: Not for me! We're off to Glacier Point.

MUIR: Enjoy your party, commissioners.

(Roosevelt, Muir, Leonard, and Liedig leave. The commissioners look at each other in dismay.)

COMMISSIONER 1: What do we do now?

COMMISSIONER 2: Don't worry. I've been up to Glacier Point. When the President comes back, he'll be so happy to see civilization that he'll listen to anything we say.

ACT 3

★★★★★ **SCENE 1: Nighttime. The two rangers, Muir, and Teddy Roosevelt sit around a campfire.**

NARRATOR: It looks as if the commissioner was wrong. Watching Teddy Roosevelt warm his hands by the fire and breathe deeply, it's hard to imagine that he'll be glad to leave Glacier Point. He seems as at home in the outdoors as Muir and the two rangers do.

ROOSEVELT: Charlie, you make the best cup of coffee I've ever tasted.

MUIR: You're not sorry you didn't stay at the hotel?

ROOSEVELT: And miss one of Charlie's steak dinners? No, sir! (He sips his coffee and looks around happily.) Muir, this is the most amazing place I've ever seen.

MUIR: I feel the same way. Half Dome and El Capitan still take my breath away every time I see them.

ROOSEVELT: And you think that a river of living ice—a glacier—carved it all? Well, however it happened, I feel very small.

MUIR: We could end up destroying it. Look around, Mr. President. This may be the last time you see Yosemite like this. We need the federal government to step in and create a system of parks that everyone can enjoy.

ROOSEVELT: Now, Muir, we need roads here and Charlie and Archie have got to live somewhere, don't they? So there have to be some buildings—

MUIR: Right now, Mr. President, greedy people want to log the trees; they want to build huge hotels inside the valley; they want to let sheep graze in the meadows. Sheep eat the grasses and flowers so close to the ground that they'll destroy the meadows—

ROOSEVELT: Gifford Pinchot says that sheep grazing doesn't hurt the meadows. Like you, he's a respected conservationist—

MUIR: He's wrong! He knows the truth, but he's trying to please the ranchers! He is no friend of the parks!

ROOSEVELT: I see your point, Muir, but I can also see the other side of the coin.

MUIR: I'm sorry for losing my temper, but we have no right to think that nature is here to be used. We're *part* of nature—only a part.

ROOSEVELT: I agree with you, Muir. Now, let's put some more wood on that fire.

NARRATOR: Instead of getting more wood for the fire, Muir goes off quietly and lights a huge dead tree in the meadow. When he returns to the President, the blaze is awesome.

ROOSEVELT: Hurray! That's a candle it took 500 years to make! Hurray! Hurray for Yosemite!

SCENE 2: Dawn. The third day of the camping trip. Snow has fallen overnight.

ROOSEVELT (shaking the snow from his blankets and laughing): Wake up, Muir! There must be four inches of snow on you.

MUIR: Good morning . . . how did you sleep?

ROOSEVELT: Like a baby. I didn't think the valley could get any more beautiful, but I was wrong. Look at it all dressed in snow.

MUIR: It smells like Charlie's cooking up some ham and eggs.

ROOSEVELT: Let's eat quickly and head out. I'm anxious to see how the valley looks in the snow.

NARRATOR: The four men broke camp just before dawn and rode off to Glacier Point.

SCENE 3: Dawn at Glacier Point.

ROOSEVELT: What a magnificent sunrise. Look at the valley . . . covered in snow . . . it looks like it's shining from the inside out. It's simply amazing.

MUIR: Look over there sir. That's Overhanging Rock. It's got a straight drop of 3,500 feet to the valley.

ROOSEVELT: Can we get to it? Can we get to the top of it?

NARRATOR: Throughout the rest of the day on the trail, Muir did most of the talking, filling the President's head with ideas of expanding Yosemite, creating a system of national parks in the United States and preserving nature. When the camping trip came to an end, Roosevelt felt rested and happy. He was ready to go back to politics.

ACT 4

★★★★★ **SCENE:** *Sentinel Bridge in the valley floor. A crowd of reporters and politicians are watching Roosevelt, Muir, and the two rangers approach.*

MUIR: Well, Mr. President there's Stoneman House. That's a sure sign that we're close to civilization.

ROOSEVELT: When you compare that thing to the magnificent natural formations all around, it looks like it doesn't belong.

MUIR: It doesn't belong, and if you don't do something about it, a lot more hotels will be popping up in the valley.

ROOSEVELT (smiling as he comes closer to the waiting crowd): Don't worry, Muir. I've heard you. I had no choice. You're the only one who can outtalk me!

COMMISSIONER 2 (to the Governor of California and Commissioner 4): Everything's ready. We're planning fireworks tonight. It'll be a great party—colored searchlights bouncing all over the place—it'll be spectacular!

GOVERNOR: I don't think the President will go for that.

COMMISSIONER 4: I don't think so either.

COMMISSIONER 2 (winking at Commissioners 1 and 3): I guess the President pretty much likes what *we* like—

COMMISSIONER 3: Ssh! Here he comes!

COMMISSIONER 2: Welcome, Mr. President. You must be so tired. I've been up to Glacier Point, and I *know*—

ROOSEVELT (in an excited tone): Tired?! Not me! Why, just last night we were in a snowstorm, and it was just what I wanted!

REPORTER (to Commissioner 2): I've been covering Teddy for years. I don't think I've ever seen him so . . . happy.

COMMISSIONER 2 (ignoring the reporter): I *know* you're hungry, Mr. President. We have a buffet waiting for you.

ROOSEVELT (ignoring Commissioner 2): Not hungry. No, this is my last night here. What about it, Muir? Think you can stand one more night out in the wild? Where's Archie? Hold on, Charlie! Don't unpack your gear!

COMMISSIONER 3 (sounding desperate): But we have fireworks planned—and, and a light show, and—

NARRATOR: Muir, Roosevelt, and the two rangers camped by themselves the last

night. The next day, the President returned to Washington, but he and Muir remained lifelong friends. From that day on, not another giant tree was cut down in Yosemite valley, and sheep were banned from the valley's meadows. In time, with the help of Governor George Pardee, Yosemite valley became part of Yosemite National Park, which was enlarged and protected forever by the federal government. In later years, President Roosevelt created other national parks. And that's how John Muir became the father of our national parks.

John Muir
Teaching Guide

Born in Dunbar, Scotland, on April 21, 1838, John Muir immigrated to America with his family when he was eleven years old. Muir attended the University of Wisconsin; but, despite being a brilliant student, he left without earning a degree to travel and find his true calling. After a factory accident nearly cost him his eye, Muir had an epiphany of sorts: He dedicated himself to "the university of the wilderness." In 1868, he explored the high country of the Sierra Nevada mountain range, including Yosemite valley, and fell in love with it. Muir called the mountains "the range of light." In Yosemite he formulated his then controversial glacial theories. After marrying in 1880, he and Louie settled in California. Muir's wife and two daughters shared his passions; the girls, expert horsewomen, often accompanied their father on his mountain treks. In 1913, Muir and the Sierra Club lost the battle for Hetch valley in California, which some naturalists considered more sublime than Yosemite. The valley was dammed and became part of the San Francisco reservoir system. According to close friends, the loss shattered Muir. This defeat, coupled with his failing health, led to his death the following year. John Muir Day is celebrated in California and in other states every April 21.

Book Links

Son of the Wilderness: The Life of John Muir by Linnie Marsh Wolfe (Knopf, 1978)

Kidding Around the National Parks of the Southwest: A Young Person's Guide Sarah Lovett (John Muir Publications, 1990)

John Muir: Wilderness Protector by Ginger Wadworth (Lerner Publications, 1992)

EXTENSION ACTIVITIES

Talk About It

★ **MAN VS NATURE?:** John Muir said man revolves around nature, not the other way around. He believed that people are a part of nature not separate from it. Ask students if they think other living things have just as much right to exist as humans. How do they feel about clear cutting of forests, building dams, strip mining, and the raising of animals for fur coats? What are the benefits and the drawbacks to nature—including humans—of each of these practices? In their opinions, do the benefits outweigh the drawbacks? If not, what do they think can be done to change the balance?

☆ **OUR FAVORITE PARKS:** Today, there are national park sites in both rural and urban areas. Open a discussion about national parks, and find out which national parks or forests students have visited. If possible, have them bring in photographs, postcards, or mementos from their trips to share with the class. What were the students' favorite places within the parks? Were the parks crowded? Do they think John Muir would be pleased by the way in which the national parks have been preserved? What might the areas within the national parks be like today if John Muir hadn't talked Teddy Roosevelt into protecting the land?

Write About It

☆ **GREEN NEWSPAPERS:** Who are the environmental heroes in your community? Which environmental issues concern people in your area? Turn your students into roving newspaper reporters and your classroom into a newsroom. Ask everyone to contribute one article, drawing, and/or photograph that documents the environmental issues about which they feel strongly. Bring in a local newspaper and point out the different types of news writing it contains: news stories, editorials, letters to the editors, political cartoons, and sections about people (interviews, births, parties, weddings, deaths), sports, and entertainment. When the class newspaper has been published, you may wish to suggest that students sell copies of it and invest in saving the Amazon rain forest. The Audobon Society sponsors a program in Belize, South America: for a fifty-dollar donation, one acre of rain forest will be held in trust for the donor. The land will be preserved, and the donor receives a certificate of ownership.

☆ **MAKE A MUIR DAY:** In 1988, California proclaimed April 21 as John Muir Day. If your state does not have a John Muir Day, invite students to start a letter-writing campaign to your Congressional representatives asking them to recognize Muir's accomplishments. Before they compose their letters, tell students to think not only about John Muir's deeds but also about how his actions have directly affected their own lives.

Be sure to give students opportunities to share their writing via read-alouds, bulletin boards, writing walls, learning centers, and so on.

Report About It

☆ **ANOTHER POINT OF VIEW:** Until 1851 the Yosemite valley was home to the Ahwahneeches, a Native American tribe. Ask students to find out more about the Ahwahneeches. How did they use the land? Bring in a photograph of Yosemite and ask students to write a poem about the image from the point of view of an Ahwahneeche.

☆ **GLACIER MODELS:** John Muir postulated that a huge glacier carved out Yosemite valley. Ask students to research how glaciers formed Yosemite. Rather than presenting their findings in written form, students can use physical models or draw diagrams to illustrate the glaciers' impact.

Thomas Edison and Alexander Graham Bell
A Meeting of Two Minds

by Meish Goldish

Characters (in order of appearance):

NARRATOR

THOMAS ALVA EDISON

ALEXANDER GRAHAM BELL

THOMAS WATSON: Bell's assistant

SPECTATORS 1-3

JOHN KRUESI: Edison's shop foreman

WORKERS 1-3

ACT 1

★★★★★ **SCENE: 1920. The compartment of a passenger train traveling from Boston to Washington, D.C. Thomas Alva Edison is walking down the corridor. He stops when he sees Bell sitting in a compartment.**

NARRATOR: The year 1847 was a lucky one for America. In that single year, two of the country's greatest inventors were born. On February 11, Thomas Alva Edison arrived. Then, on March 3, Alexander Graham Bell came into the world. During their lives, they pursued similar projects. The funny thing is, these two men never met and so they never worked together. Let's imagine what Thomas Edison and Alexander Graham Bell might have said to each other had their paths crossed.

EDISON: Pardon me, but aren't you Alexander Graham Bell?

BELL: Yes, I am.

EDISON: Thomas Alva Edison.

(Edison holds out his hand. He and Bell shake hands.)

BELL: I'm very glad to meet you, sir. Please, sit down

EDISON (sitting down): What's that? I'm afraid you'll have to speak up. I'm partially deaf. When I was a child, a railroad conductor pulled on my ears. My hearing has grown worse ever since.

BELL: I'm very sorry to hear that. I've spent much of my life working with the deaf. In fact, I ran a school for teachers of the deaf in Boston.

EDISON: Boston! Why, I was in Boston, operating a telegraph, in 1868.

BELL: Really! I didn't get there till four years later. But Mr. Edison—

EDISON: Please, call me Alva. All my family and friends call me by my middle name.

BELL: Amazing! Another coincidence! My friends and relatives call me Graham, which is my middle name! I'm curious, Alva. If you're hard of hearing, how in the world did you manage to invent the phonograph?

EDISON: I listened through my skull. I put my head against the phonograph speaker and heard everything perfectly well. In fact, being deaf has been an advantage for me. It's easier to concentrate sometimes.

BELL: Amazing!

EDISON: Now I have a question, Graham. How did a teacher of the deaf come to invent the telephone?

BELL: It's an interesting story. And believe it or not, it all began with my experiments on a telegraph, back in 1875. Let me set the scene for you.

92

ACT 2

⭐⭐⭐⭐⭐ SCENE 1: 1875. Bell's laboratory in Boston. He and Thomas Watson are sitting in different rooms.

BELL: Mr. Watson, you are a most valuable assistant. You've been a great help making the electrical parts for the telegraph.

WATSON: Thank you, Mr. Bell. I hope this experiment is a success.

BELL: I do, too, Watson. The telegraph is proof that noise and signals can be sent over electrified wires, and so it seems to me that human speech can be sent over telegraph wires, as well. Yet all the tests have failed so far.

WATSON: I'll check the reeds on the telegraph once more.

NARRATOR: Watson plucks a reed. In the other room, Bell hears the sound over the wire. At first, he can't believe he's heard the sound. Watson plucks another reed. Bell jumps off his stool and runs in excitement to the other room.

BELL: Watson! What did you do just then? Don't change anything!

NARRATOR: That breakthrough, on June 2, 1875, encouraged Bell to keep working on his telephone. On March 7 of the following year, Bell and Watson were experimenting in separate rooms, trying out a new transmitter. Suddenly, Bell spilled battery acid on his clothing.

BELL: Mr. Watson, come here! I want you!

WATSON (rushes into room)**:** Mr. Bell! It works! I heard your voice perfectly over the wire! You said, "Mr. Watson, come here! I want you!"

BELL: So, human speech can travel by wire after all! My telephone works!

SCENE 2: 1876. Exposition in Philadelphia. Bell is standing in front of a booth, demonstrating the telephone.

SPECTATOR 1: Mr. Bell, you're a genius!

SPECTATOR 2: Now I'll be able to talk to my son in California—(snaps his fingers) just like that!

SPECTATOR 3: Mr. Bell, what do you plan to do next?

BELL: I'd like to go back to helping the deaf.

SCENE 3: 1920. The train's dining car. Edison and Bell are seated together at a table.

EDISON: And is that what you did, Graham?

BELL: That's exactly what I did. I used the money I made from the telephone to set up a lab. I did research on deafness, and I kept inventing. I found a way to make phonograph records on wax discs in my lab.

EDISON: You made the discs, and I made the phonograph to play them on!

BELL: So you did, Alva. You know, I'd really like to hear how you got your phonograph to work.

EDISON: Well, Graham, it happened in 1877, the year after your telephone invention. Now, let *me* set the scene for *you!*

ACT 3
★★★★★ SCENE: 1877. At laboratory in Menlo Park, New Jersey, Edison sits at a table with John Kruesi, the shop foreman.

EDISON: John, I sure hope this new contraption succeeds. I know a lot of people around here think the idea of recorded sound is crazy.

KRUESI: They think you'll fail, but you can't listen to them.

EDISON: Let them think it. To my mind, there's no such thing as failure. If an experiment doesn't succeed the first 10,000 times, it doesn't mean I've failed. I've just found 10,000 ways that won't work!

KRUESI: What are you hoping will happen this time?

EDISON: Take a look, John. I've got a funnel here. At the other end is a paper cutout of a man with a saw and a log. Now here comes the test. (He shouts into the funnel.) "Mary had a little lamb. Its fleece was white as snow." (pause) Look, John! The paper man is sawing the wood! My voice waves made him move. Now I'm sure I can make a recording of those waves!

NARRATOR: Edison drew a sketch of the machine he wanted, and John Kruesi built it. The machine had a cylinder like a tin can with tinfoil wrapped around it. Soon the time came to test the phonograph. All the workers in Edison's shop watched closely.

WORKER 1: What's this thing going to do, Alva?

EDISON: Talk—this machine is going to talk.

WORKER 2 (laughing): Talk! That's a good one! A talking machine!

EDISON (leaning into the mouthpiece): "Mary had a little lamb. Its fleece was white as snow."

(There is silence. Then all the workers laugh.)

94

WORKER 3 (whispering to co-workers): Looks like recorded sound is a fool's dream after all.

EDISON: Let's try it once more. (He adjusts the tinfoil slightly before speaking into the mouthpiece again.) "Mary had a little lamb. Its fleece was white as snow." (This time, the machine plays back Edison's words.)

WORKER 1: I can't believe it! Your phonograph works! It actually works!

ALL WORKERS (singing): For he's a jolly good genius, for he's a jolly good genius, for he's a jolly good genius—which nobody can deny!

ACT 4
★★★★★ SCENE: 1920. The train compartment. Edison and Bell have returned to the compartment to continue their talk.

BELL: So, Alva, after the experiment worked, they called you a genius.

EDISON: Some say that genius is a gift, but I don't think so. You know as well as I do that it's mostly hard work. I've always believed that genius is one percent inspiration and 99 percent perspiration.

BELL: Very true, Alva. You know, I learned a similar lesson with the telephone. My first experiments failed, but I kept testing, over and over, until it finally worked.

EDISON: I'm very proud that I was able to continue work on your telephone and improve on it a little.

BELL: That's right. You did!

EDISON: Your telephone was a fine piece of work, Graham, but people had to shout into it in order to be heard on the other end. Adding a carbon transmitter helped. Maybe we should call it the "Edison telephone" instead of the "Bell telephone."

(Both men laugh.)

BELL: Remember, Alva, that I improved the phonograph after you invented it. I made records that were round and flat. They could hold more sound than your tin-can cylinder.

EDISON: That's true, Graham. You did.

BELL: It's funny. I always wanted to be remembered as a teacher of the deaf. Americans remember me as the inventor of the telephone instead.

EDISON: I wouldn't complain. We've both been praised and honored by Americans and by other people all over the world.

BELL: Oh, I'm not complaining. But I do admit it's harder to work in my laboratory these days. I keep getting interrupted—by telephone calls!

Thomas Edison and Alexander Graham Bell
Teaching Guide

Thomas Alva Edison was born on February 11, 1847, in Milan, Ohio. His strong curiosity and constant questions annoyed his teacher, and Thomas left school after only three months. He was taught by his mother and read many books on his own. Edison's first invention, in 1868, was an electric vote-recording machine. Later, he improved the stock ticker and made enough money to establish a laboratory for his experiments. Edison devoted his life to his work and patented over a thousand inventions, including the electric light, the phonograph, and motion pictures. He died in 1931. Alexander Graham Bell was born on March 3, 1847, in Edinburgh, Scotland. His father, a teacher of the deaf, deeply influenced Alexander. He went on to assist his father in that work. When Alexander's health became threatened in 1870, the family moved to Canada. Later Alexander settled in Boston, where he opened a school for teachers of the deaf. In 1877, he married Mabel Hubbard, who was deaf. Bell's invention of the telephone, patented in 1876, led the way immediately to telephone service in America and England. Bell continued working with the deaf while developing other inventions. He became an American citizen in 1882, and died in 1922.

Book Links

Thomas Alva Edison: Great Inventor by David Adler (Holiday House, 1990)

Thomas Edison: Inventing the Future by Penny Mintz (Fawcett Columbine, 1989)

The Story of Alexander Graham Bell: Inventor of the Telephone by Margaret Davidson (Dell, 1989)

Alexander Graham Bell by Andrew Dunn (Bookwright Press, 1991)

Thomas Edison-Alexander Graham Bell by Naunerle C. Farr (Pendulum Press, 1979)

EXTENSION ACTIVITIES

Talk About It

☆ **INVENTIONS WE LOVE:** Bell gave us the telephone and Edison the light bulb.

Ask students to list the five greatest inventions ever created. Then have them read their lists aloud while you make one cumulative list on the board. Let the class tally the inventions that are repeated. Determine how many students named the telephone or the phonograph as being among the greatest inventions. Discuss why they feel these inventions are so important to society. How would the world be different today if the telephone and sound recordings didn't exist?

☆ **A FAX FOR ALVA:** What would the two inventors think of modern technology? Have students work in cooperative groups of four or five. Invite them to discuss these questions: In what ways were Thomas Alva Edison and Alexander Graham Bell similar? What details in their lives were parallel? How were their attitudes about work alike? What differences did you discover between the two men from reading the play? How do you think each man would react to modern technology such as VCRs, cellular telephones, and personal computers? Which of the two men do you admire more, and why?

Write About It

☆ **1% INSPIRATION:** Thomas Edison said, "Genius is one percent inspiration and 99 perspiration." Invite students to write their own definitions for the word *genius*. Then have them describe someone they know or know about who fits their definitions and to explain their decisions. It might be another inventor, for example, or perhaps a politician or teacher.

☆ **EFFORT ESSAYS:** Both Edison and Bell strongly believed in persistence, even after repeated failure. Ask students to write about personal experiences where they had to keep trying in order to succeed. What were their ultimate goals? What difficulties stood in their way? How did they finally manage to reach their goals?

Be sure to give students opportunities to share their writing via read-alouds, bulletin boards, writing walls, learning centers, and so on.

Report About It

☆ **BE AN INVENTOR:** Now it's your students' turn to invent something. Inspire their creative thinking by asking them to think of tasks they wish were easier or faster. Encourage them to walk around their homes, and interview their parents to get ideas. Students can present models, diagrams, or descriptions of their inventions to the class.

☆ **INVENTIVE TIME LINE:** Alexander Graham Bell and Thomas Edison were born in the same year. Have inventors and their inventions flourished at certain periods of time in human history? Ask students to research the exact years that important inventions were patented or, if there are not detailed records, when it is supposed that the invention was recognized. Have the class present the information in the form of a time line. Students may use long sheets of mural paper to create their time lines and then display their work on the classroom walls.

George Washington Carver

The Scientist Who Saved the South

by Adam Grant

Characters (in order of appearance):

NARRATORS 1-2

AUNT SUSAN CARVER

UNCLE MOSES CARVER

GEORGE WASHINGTON CARVER

MRS. KAYDEN: A neighbor

SCHOOLTEACHER

BOOKER T. WASHINGTON

STUDENTS 1-3

FARMERS 1-2

COMMUNITY LEADER

ACT 1

NARRATOR 1: George Washington Carver was born into slavery in 1864 during the Civil War. He lived in Missouri on a small farm where his mother Mary was a slave to the Carver family.

NARRATOR 2: Near the end of the war, Mary and her children were kidnapped. A search party found George but no one else. The Carvers took George, who was a small and sickly baby, and raised him. He called them Uncle Moses and Aunt Susan. The Carvers cared for George as if he were their son. Soon he grew into a healthy, intelligent little boy. Almost from the time he could talk, George showed a keen interest in plants and flowers.

AUNT SUSAN: Moses, have you seen what George has done to my geraniums?

UNCLE MOSES: What do you mean?

AUNT SUSAN: A few days ago, I saw him crouching over those scrawny little plants by the back porch. Just look at them now! I swear they're the most beautiful flowers in the county.

UNCLE MOSES: Well, how about that? George, come on out here a minute!

(George comes out the front door of the farmhouse.)

GEORGE: Yes, Uncle Moses?

UNCLE MOSES: What have you been doing to these flowers out here?

GEORGE: Loving them.

UNCLE MOSES: Loving them! What do you mean?

GEORGE: They looked lonely, so I went over and talked to them. While we were talking, I noticed some bugs under the leaves, so I took them off. I think the geraniums feel a lot better now.

UNCLE MOSES: While you were talking to the plants . . . ?

GEORGE: The flowers talked to me, not with words exactly, but I could hear them. You could hear them too, if you listened close.

AUNT SUSAN: Well, whatever it is you did, George, my geraniums have never looked better. You come out here and talk to them all you want. (looking around the yard) Hmm, maybe you should have a word with my roses.

SCENE 2: 1870s. Mrs. Kayden's front yard. She is a neighbor of the Carvers.

NARRATOR 1: Soon George was known around the area as "the plant doctor." He spent most afternoons at neighbors's houses, tending to their plants for nickels or for small treats.

MRS. KAYDEN: George, how come my roses aren't as pretty as you all's?

GEORGE: They're in the wrong place. Roses love the sun.

MRS. KAYDEN: Show me where I should put them. Then we can have some hot blueberry turnovers before we transplant those rosebushes.

(George lifts his face to the sky and walks to a sunny spot in the yard. He stops.)

GEORGE: If I were a rose, I'd be happy right here.

ACT 2
★★★★★★ **SCENE: Diamond Grove, Missouri. George and Uncle Moses are standing in front of the schoolhouse.**

NARRATOR 2: George loved to spend time studying plants in the woods, learning all he could about them. He wished he could do nothing but learn all day long. When he saw the town school, George couldn't believe his eyes. He wanted to attend more than anything in the whole world.

GEORGE: I can't wait till I'm big enough to go to school. Do you think they'd let me in next fall, Uncle Moses?

UNCLE MOSES: George . . . you can't go to that school.

GEORGE: Why? What do you mean?

UNCLE MOSES: It's for white children. You can't go there.

GEORGE: Where do I go to school then?

UNCLE MOSES: I'm sorry, George. There's not a school for you. I wish you could go here, but it's against the law.

GEORGE: But I want to go to school! I want to learn how to read and write and do sums!

UNCLE MOSES: Tell you what—I can teach you to read and your Aunt Susan can teach you your sums. How about that?

GEORGE: Can you teach me everything the white kids learn?

UNCLE MOSES: Well . . . I'm pretty sure we can.

100

NARRATOR 1: George couldn't understand why he couldn't attend the white school. There were red roses and yellow roses, but the color didn't matter. Everybody knew that they were all roses. Why was it any different with people?

ACT 3
★★★★★ **SCENE 1: Small house in rural Missouri, the site of a school for black students. George and the schoolteacher are standing in front.**

NARRATOR 2: Despite the Carvers's lessons, George knew the only way he was ever going to get an education was to find schools that were for black people. Most of the schools he discovered had little money and were very small. It took George only a few years to outgrow each school. He'd learn everything he could, and then he'd have to leave to find another school.

NARRATOR 1: Sometimes George had to work years at a time, doing laundry or cooking, just to make enough money to pay for the next school. Sometimes, when he went to a new town, the racial prejudice was so strong that he would be chased out before he could even settle down.

SCHOOLTEACHER: I'm sorry to lose you, George. You're my best student. You keep me on my toes.

GEORGE: I appreciate all you've taught me, sir. I'll miss our talks.

SCHOOLTEACHER: I don't know how my tomatoes are going to hold up with you gone.

GEORGE (laughing and waving good-bye): Don't forget to stake them up, and they'll be fine.

SCENE 2: The grounds of Tuskegee Institute in Alabama.

NARRATOR 2: Finally, after being turned down by many colleges, George was accepted to study at Simpson College in Iowa and then at Iowa State College. Soon, he was renowned as a teacher and a scientist. Carver's specialty was inventing and teaching new farming techniques. His greatest challenges came when he agreed to teach at the new Tuskegee Institute, a college for black students in Alabama.

NARRATOR 1: When Carver arrived at Tuskegee, the school's president, Booker T. Washington, showed him around the small school. There was little to see except for a building in bad shape sitting on a dirt lot.

WASHINGTON: Welcome, Dr. Carver. We're very honored to have you here. We're very poor, as you can see. One day Tuskegee will be a great university, but right now we'll all have to pitch in to make it grow.

CARVER (kneeling down and taking a handful of soil)**:** The soil is quite poor here, but I can fix that once I've had time to study it in the lab. The harder we work here, the better off our people will be.

(The two men walk toward the building.)

WASHINGTON: I knew you were just the man we needed here! We need your spirit! Well, here we are. Welcome to your new laboratory.

NARRATOR 2: Dr. Carver looked inside the building. There was only one room, and it was empty.

CARVER: This is going to be quite a challenge.

SCENE 3: Inside Carver's classroom and lab at Tuskegee.

NARRATOR 1: On the first day of class about thirteen young men walked into the empty room where Dr. Carver was to hold his lectures.

STUDENT 1: I'm sorry, sir. I'm looking for the farming science class.

CARVER: This is it. Don't sit down yet. We're going on a scavenger hunt.

STUDENT 2: Sir? A scavenger hunt? What are we looking for?

CARVER: A laboratory!

STUDENT 3: I don't get it.

CARVER: I want you all to go out and bring back everything you find that you think we can use. When you get back, we'll see what we've got.

NARRATOR 1: When the students returned, they had all kinds of things including pots and pans and old tin cans and soda bottles.

CARVER: You all found some terrific stuff! We can use these bottles for test tubes, and this old pot can be our stove.

NARRATOR 2: Soon, Dr. Carver and his students had made their own lab, and they could get down to the business of farming science. Dr. Carver taught them how to grow certain crops that would replace the nutrients that years of cotton farming had taken from the soil. The students learned how to make the most of the crops they grew so that more people could be fed.

NARRATOR 1: Before long, Dr. Carver and his class were able to take their lessons on the road. They traveled all over Alabama and the rest of the South, helping farmers and learning more and more. By now, George Washington Carver was the most respected farming scientist in the country. His fame was so widespread that two presidents, William McKinley and Theodore Roosevelt, visited him.

ACT 4
★★★★★ SCENE 1: Carver's experimental fields at Tuskegee Institute.

NARRATOR 2: Farming was the biggest industry in the South, and most southern farmers grew cotton. Suddenly, the cotton fields were hit by a mysterious ailment. So many plants died that it looked as if the farmers would go broke and their families might starve.

NARRATOR 1: It was soon discovered that the cotton was dying because of tiny bugs called boll weevils, which ate cotton and laid millions of eggs in the plants. Panic spread across the land. The South was headed for disaster.

CARVER: Those boll weevils aren't going anywhere. Everybody's trying to figure out how to get rid of them, but that's useless. Most of the cotton is already dead. What I've got to do is find another crop that people can grow—a crop the boll weevil won't eat.

NARRATOR 2: Dr. Carver looked at his own fields planted with experimental crops. The peanuts were healthy and robust and showed no signs of boll weevil damage.

CARVER: Peanuts! How am I going to get people to grow peanuts? Nobody eats them unless they go to a circus. Then the elephant gets most of them. Peanuts! What uses can I find for them?

NARRATOR 1: Dr. Carver shut himself in his lab and learned everything he could about the peanut. What he found out pleased him, and soon he called several important farmers together to tell them about his discovery.

FARMER 1 (looking at the peanut field): Are you crazy? You expect some stupid nut to replace King Cotton? Can you wear them? No! Can you sit down and make a meal of them? No! Sure, we can grow 'em, but who'll we sell 'em to?

CARVER: You can't sit down and eat cotton, either. Peanuts aren't nuts, they're from an herb family. They're very nutritious—

FARMER 2: They may not be nuts, but you sure are! I'm not plowing my cotton under to make room for any peanuts.

SCENE 2: The faculty dining room at Tuskegee Institute.

NARRATOR 2: Dr. Carver knew that if he and the peanut were going to save the South, he was going to have to find many more ways to use and sell the new crop. He went back to his lab and worked for months. No one was allowed to visit him or see what he was working on. At last, Carver invited community leaders and farmers to a special dinner to unveil his project.

CARVER: Welcome, welcome. Glad you could all come. I hope you all are hungry! I've prepared a very special meal for you. We have soup, chicken, ice cream, and cookies!

(Everyone sits down and begins to eat. Carver watches the leaders closely to see how they like the food.)

LEADER: Great chicken! But what does all this have to do with your project? Something about peanuts, wasn't it?

CARVER: Yes. In fact, everything you're eating has been made with peanuts. That's all I used. Even the "chicken" is really made with peanuts. There are hundreds of other uses for the peanut, too. I've taken apart the peanut chemically and found hundreds of things that you can make from the different parts—metal polish, new building materials, shampoo, paper, varnish, paint—even milk! The peanut is going to create so much new business that you won't even miss cotton.

LEADER: The soup? That's made out of peanuts, too? What do you know! Now listen here, Dr. Carver, I know you're sold on the peanut, but—

FARMER: Why are we eating something a boll weevil won't even touch?

CARVER: The best news for you, sir, is that the peanut plant is so good for the soil you can plant it year after year!

FARMER: Well, why didn't you say so? Pass that chicken!

NARRATOR 1: George Washington Carver had done it! He had used science to save the South. In later years, he went on to invent hundreds of other things and to enrich the lives of thousands of young people as a teacher.

NARRATOR 2: Dr. Carver was very old when he died. All over America, people mourned him. Carver had improved the world more than almost any other person of his generation. At a time when ignorance and misunderstanding created racism and cruelty in America, he used his enormous talents and strength of character to better the lives of all people.

George Washington Carver
Teaching Guide

George Washington Carver was born a slave on a farm in Diamond Grove, Missouri, in 1864. The exact date of his birth is unknown. His mother Mary was kidnapped from the farm during the Civil War. George was raised by the Carvers, his former master and mistress, almost as a son. A potential victim of the Jim Crow system in the antebellum South, Carver had to work diligently to receive an education. He attended college in Iowa, first at Simpson College and then at Iowa State. Carver became a professor of science at Iowa State, but soon moved on to Booker T. Washington's new Tuskegee Institute, a black university in Alabama. Carver was invited to speak in Congress and he met several presidents. His greatest contributions were in teaching poor southern farmers how to avert starvation through farming science. He revitalized the boll-weevil-ridden South with the introduction of the peanut and the myriad synthetics that could be created from it. After a long life of selfless service to his community and the world, Carver died in his eighties at Tuskegee.

Book Links

George Washington Carver: The Man Who Overcame by Lawrence Elliott (Prentice-Hall, 1966)

George Washington Carver: Agricultural Scientist by Sam and Beryl Epstein (Dell Yearling, 1991)

George Washington Carver: Nature's Trailblazer by Teresa Rogers (TFC Books, 1992)

EXTENSION ACTIVITIES

Talk About It

☆ **CONSIDERING CARVER'S CHILDHOOD:** George Washington Carver's last name came from the people who owned him and his mother. Talk about the circumstances in which Carver was brought up. How do students feel about Aunt Susan and Uncle Moses? Were they surprised that the Carvers took in and cared for George after his mother died? What kinds of advantages and disadvantages do students think George experienced because of growing up as an accepted member of a white household? How might that have made life easier for him? Harder?

☆ **WHEN TWO CAREERS CONVERGE:** People deal with prejudice in many different ways. Carver chose to work as hard as he could and make an example of himself to all whom he encountered. Booker T. Washington established a school for African American students. What would have happened if either man had chosen a different path? Ask students to create verbal scenarios about what might have happened to Carver if there had not been a Tuskegee Institute and what might have happened to Washington if Carver had not come to Tuskegee.

Write About It

☆ **NATURE LEARNING LABS:** George Washington Carver began his education at an early age. White schools might have barred him, but the woods never did. Let students create a nature learning lab in the classroom. They may plant flower seeds in a paper cup filled with potting soil or another medium; wrap dried pinto or lima beans in a wet paper towel and then place the towel inside a glass jar; or stick toothpicks in a sweet potato or avocado pit and suspend it in a jar of water. Ask students to keep a journal of their plants' progress. Encourage them to incorporate drawings into their entries.

☆ **THANK YOU LETTERS:** If it weren't for George Washington Carver, former President Jimmy Carter might not have been a peanut farmer. He might not have had a farm at all. After students consider the various ways in which Carver extended the use of the peanut, ask them which ones they appreciate the most and why. Have them write a thank-you letter to Carver.

Be sure to give students opportunities to share their writing via read-alouds, bulletin boards, writing walls, learning centers, and so on.

Report About It

☆ **APPRECIATING TUSKEGEE:** Booker T. Washington and Tuskegee Institute played an important role in George Washington Carver's career and life. What is the history of Tuskegee Institute and how did Booker T. Washington come to found it? Ask students to find out more about Washington or Tuskegee Institute and prepare a report. Encourage creativity in the way in which the material is presented; for example, some students may wish to write a play based upon Washington's life or the period of time when he founded Tuskegee or they may present a pictorial essay using photographs and their own drawings to chronicle the growth of Tuskegee and some of its graduates.

☆ **CARVER SCIENCE FAIR:** Carver's work substantially affected people's lives. What are some of his other discoveries? After in-depth research, ask students to select one discovery on which to report; they may work in pairs or small groups. Hold a George Washington Carver Appreciation Day and Science Fair in your classroom. To emphasize the hands-on, scientific aspect of this activity, you may wish to ask a science teacher to serve as a consultant. If other classes are invited to the event, encourage students to perform the play so guests will learn more about Carver.

Susan LaFlesche Picotte
An Omaha Doctor Returns Home

by Jacqueline Charlesworth

Characters (in order of appearance):

NARRATOR

SUSAN LAFLESCHE (lah-FLESH) **PICOTTE** (pea-COT)

IRON EYE (Joseph LaFlesche): Susan's father

ROSALIE: Susan's older sister

CROWD OF PEOPLE 1-5

THOMAS FOX: an Omaha man

RESERVATION DOCTOR

SAM FOX

GOVERNMENT AGENT

FEMALE STUDENT

DOCTOR MARTHA WALDRON

MALE STUDENTS 1-3

SURGEON

ACT 1

SCENE: Late 1800s. An Omaha village on the Nebraska prairie. There are new wooden houses mixed in with the traditional tepees. Joseph LaFlesche, known to the Omaha as Chief Iron Eye, is walking through the village. At his side is his teenage daughter Rosalie.

NARRATOR: In 1850, there were 50 million buffalo roaming the vast prairies of North America. By 1883, after white people had moved west and hunted the buffalo on a massive scale, only 50 remained. The loss of the buffalo meant the end of the traditional way of life for the Omaha and other Plains Indians who depended on the animal for food and clothing. These Native Americans were forced to relocate to reservations, land set aside for them by the U.S. government. There, they were supervised by government officials. Confined to reservations, often with little food, many people grew sick.

(Susan runs up to her father and her older sister.)

SUSAN: Father, come quick! There's trouble at the doctor's!

IRON EYE: Slow down. Tell me what you know.

SUSAN (trying to catch her breath): It's Thomas Fox! He's got the doctor and he won't let him go!

ROSALIE: There'll be trouble if the agent finds out.

IRON EYE: Rosalie—go to the agent's office. If he hears anything and starts to head for the doctor's, make sure you get to the doctor's first.

NARRATOR: Rosalie hurries to the government agent's office. Iron Eye and Susan run to the doctor's office. The door to the office is locked. A crowd of people are standing outside the office.

PERSON 1: My child is sick, too! Tell Thomas Fox to let the doctor go!

PERSON 2: Why don't you talk louder? That way the government agent will be sure to hear you, and we'll all get into trouble.

PERSON 3: Let Thomas Fox have the doctor! What good does his medicine do?

PERSON 4: He made Annie's Wild Horse's cough go away, didn't he? It's not his fault we're sick.

PERSON 5: I'm not so sure about that.

IRON EYE: Go about your business—all of you. I'll settle this.

(The people walk off in different directions. Iron eye knocks on the door.)

IRON EYE: Thomas Fox, open the door!

108

THOMAS FOX (through the door): Are you alone?

IRON EYE: Yes, but I may not be alone for long.

NARRATOR: Susan heard the sound of someone coughing inside the office. The door opened slightly. Iron eye walked into the office. Susan slipped in after him. Thomas Fox's son Sam, wrapped in blankets, was lying on the examining table. The doctor was tied to his chair. Thomas Fox locked the door.

THOMAS FOX: Look at him! Look at my son! We have no meat. He hasn't had any to eat in two weeks. Feel his face! See how hot he is!

IRON EYE: How can the doctor help Sam if he's tied up?

THOMAS FOX: He said he was too busy to come and look at Sam so I brought Sam to him. Then he says he can't see my son because he has to go to someone's house—

DOCTOR: I can't see everyone at once. I have to see those who are the most ill—

THOMAS FOX: Look at my son! How much sicker does he have to get?

DOCTOR: There are people who are worse off than your son is. People who may die if you don't let me go.

IRON EYE: Thomas, let him go. He'll look at Sam. Then you take him home. Susan will bring you some meat this afternoon.

SAM (coughing): I want to go home, Dad.

(There is a quick knock on the door.)

ROSALIE (through the door): The agent's coming!

(A few seconds later, the agent knocks loudly on the door. Everyone inside the doctor's office freezes.)

AGENT (rattling the door): What's going on in there? Open up! I know you're in there, Iron Eye! You all right, Doc?

DOCTOR: I'm fine. I've got a very sick boy in here.

AGENT: Open up and let me see for myself. Or do you want me to call in the soldiers?

IRON EYE: You don't want to catch a fever, do you?

AGENT: Oh. No. But I want to see you in my office, Iron Eye. Pronto.

NARRATOR: Thomas Fox untied the doctor. He did what he could for Sam Fox. As Susan watched the doctor work, she promised herself that she would do something to help her people.

ACT 2

★★★★★ SCENE 1: Hampton Institute in Virginia. Susan is in the office of Dr. Martha Waldron.

NARRATOR: At the age of fourteen, Susan left Nebraska to attend school in Virginia. The school doctor, Doctor Martha Waldron, was one of the few women doctors at that time.

DR. WALDRON: You have a little fever, Susan. I want you to rest this weekend.

SUSAN: But I have a science test on Tuesday!

DR. WALDRON: Study in bed then. Read and then rest. I mean it.

SUSAN: Yes ma'am.

DR. WALDRON: I see from your records that you're from Nebraska. What's it like? I've never been there.

SUSAN: It's beautiful. Prairies full of grass—not too many buffalo any more. It's hard to get enough to eat. People get sick . . . I wish we had a doctor like you.

DR. WALDRON: What about you? Have you ever thought about becoming a doctor?

SUSAN: I've thought about it . . . do you think I could?

DR. WALDRON: I do. It won't be easy, but I think you could do it.

SUSAN: If I were a doctor, I could help. I could really help my people.

DR. WALDRON: It will be hard, not just the studying, but in other ways. Some people won't want you to become a doctor. They won't believe that you can because you're a woman.

SUSAN: And an Indian.

DR. WALDRON: Yes, and an Indian.

SCENE 2: The Women's Medical College in Philadelphia. A class of women students are about to witness their first operation. Several male students have been invited to attend the class, as well.

NARRATOR: Susan sent an application to the Women's Medical College in Philadelphia and waited anxiously for the reply. After what seemed like a long time, the answer came. She had been admitted! That fall, Susan settled down to the hard work of becoming a doctor.

FEMALE STUDENT: Why don't you come over to my house after class, Susan? We can have some tea and compare notes.

SUSAN: Oh, I'd like to, but I wouldn't be able to stay very long. I have so much studying to do! Sometimes I wonder if I'll ever be a doctor.

FEMALE STUDENT: You study all the time! I know you'll make it.

SUSAN: I hope so. There are a lot of people back home who need a good doctor. We don't even have a hospital out there.

NARRATOR: The male students sat a few rows ahead of Susan and her classmate. They had a few things to say about women becoming doctors.

MALE STUDENT 1: I just don't think the girls can deal with this. Do they really think they can handle seeing an operation?

MALE STUDENT 2: I bet they'll all faint dead away the minute the surgeon pulls out his scalpel.

MALE STUDENT 1: At least they let the men sit in the front rows.

MALE STUDENT 3: Shhhh! Here comes the surgeon.

SURGEON: Good afternoon, gentlemen—and ladies. I will now begin the operation. We start with an incision . . . here . . .

MALE STUDENT 1: Oh, no!!

(He faints and is carried away. Meanwhile, as the operation continues, Susan and her female colleague take careful notes.)

NARRATOR: Two years later, Susan LaFlesche became the first Native American woman to graduate from medical school.

ACT 3
★★★★★ **SCENE: Rosalie's house in Nebraska as the sun sets on a cold winter day. Outside, the wind is howling and the snow is piled high.**

NARRATOR: When she returned to Nebraska, Susan was appointed to be the new doctor for the Omaha Reservation. There was still no hospital, and she was the only doctor. Because Susan had so many patients, she was usually very tired at the end of each day.

(Rosalie hears a knock and hurries to open the door. Susan enters the house, removes her heavy coat, and stamps the snow off her boots.)

ROSALIE: Susan! You look like you're frozen!

SUSAN: I am. Thank goodness I've finished my rounds for today. I can't believe how exhausting it is to walk through all that snow.

ROSALIE: You'll feel better after you've eaten. Smell that? It's your favorite! You sit down and I'll get your plate ready.

(Rosalie goes into the kitchen. Susan settles into a chair by the fire. There is a knock on the door. Susan opens it, and Sam Fox enters.)

SAM: It's Dad, Susan! He's cut his leg and it's bleeding a lot. I didn't want to move him. Could you come and take a look at him? Please?

SUSAN: I'll get my coat.

ROSALIE (entering with a plate)**:** Susan! You're not going out again, are you?

SUSAN: Thomas Fox has hurt his leg. Keep my dinner warm until I get back, okay?

ROSALIE: At least eat some dinner before you. . .(Susan and Sam Fox leave) go.

ACT 4
★★★★★ **SCENE: 1913. A small crowd is gathered in front of a new building that sits on a hilltop on the Nebraska prairie. Susan and Sam Fox stand on the porch of the building, facing the crowd.**

NARRATOR: In the next few years, Susan married a man named Henry Picotte and had two sons. In addition to caring for her family, she continued to practice medicine and to serve as a community leader. In 1913, just two years before she died, Susan saw her biggest dream come true.

SAM (addressing the crowd)**:** Folks, today is a very important day for the Omaha Reservation. We have come here to dedicate our new hospital. We have one person to thank for it: Dr. Susan, who raised the $10,000 for the building and equipment. (turning to Susan) Dr. Susan, you've always been there when we needed you. You have been a bridge from the old ways to the new. We will never forget what you have done for us.

(The crowd applauds.)

SUSAN: You may not know this, Sam, but I became a doctor because of you. You showed me one day what needed to be done for our people. It took me a while to figure out that it meant becoming a doctor and coming back home, but here we are. This is truly a happy day, but we all deserve the credit. We've all worked together to keep our community and our spirit alive.

NARRATOR: In 1989, the Dr. Susan Picotte Memorial Hospital in Whalthill, Nebraska, was placed on the National Register of Historic Places.

Susan LaFlesche Picotte
Teaching Guide

Susan LaFlesche was born on June 17, 1865, on the Omaha Reservation in Nebraska. She was the youngest of the four daughters of Joseph LaFlesche and Mary Gale. Both Joseph and Mary were of mixed Native and European American heritage. Joseph, whose Omaha name was Iron Eye, served as chief of the Omaha from 1853 until shortly after Susan was born. While a student at the Hampton Institute in Virginia, where the school doctor was a woman, Dr. Martha Waldron, Susan decided to apply to medical school. She was accepted to the Women's Medical College in Philadelphia, Pennsylvania, and attended on a scholarship. Susan became the first Native American woman to obtain a medical degree. Following medical school, Susan returned to Nebraska, where she served as the reservation doctor. She was forced to resign from this backbreaking position after four years because of her own poor health. In 1894, she married Henry Picotte; they had two sons. With Picotte helping to care for the children, Susan was able to return to the practice of medicine. At one point, she had over 1,000 patients, both Indian and white. Despite frequent bouts of illness and the death of her husband in 1905, Susan maintained a leadership role in her community, taking up issues of public health and often representing the tribe in its dealings with the U.S. government. In 1913, she succeeded in raising the money to build a hospital on the reservation. Susan Picotte died in 1915 at the age of 50.

Book Links

Native American Doctor by Jeri Ferris (Carolrhoda Books, Inc., 1991)

Iron Eye's Family: The Children of Joseph LaFlesche by Norma Kidd Green (Johnson Publishing Co., 1969)

American Indian Women by Marion E. Gridley (Hawthorne Books, 1974)

EXTENSION ACTIVITIES

Talk About It

⭐ **GOING BEYOND STEREOTYPES:** Susan LaFlesche Picotte had to overcome the prejudices of white society with respect to Native Americans and women in order to achieve what she did. Such prejudices are often expressed through stereotypes. It is not uncommon, for instance, to see stereotypical images of Native Americans and women in movies and on television. Write the headings "Girls" and "Boys" on a blackboard. Let students talk about the possible stereotypes of each gender—for example, that all girls don't like sports while all boys do. For each stereotype, ask if it's really true, and have students point out counter examples. After discussing several stereotypes, invite students to explain how stereotypical thinking can harm individuals and societies.

☆ **BRIDGING OLD AND NEW:** Sam Fox called Susan "a bridge from the old ways to the new." Ask students what he meant by this. Have they ever felt themselves to be a "bridge" between old ways and new or, perhaps, between two different people? If so, how did or do they feel about the role? What kinds of responsibilities does the role carry?

Write About It

☆ **ROLE MODEL LETTERS:** Dr. Martha Waldron, one of the country's first women doctors, was a role model for Susan. Susan, in turn, became a role model in her community. Have students write a letter to someone—famous or nonfamous—explaining why she or he is a role model for them. Some students may wish to mail their letters.

☆ **PERSONAL ESSAYS:** When she was fourteen years old, Susan LaFlesche traveled by train from Nebraska to Virginia. Have the children discuss what she must have been feeling when she stepped off the train in Virginia. Her surroundings were different—she was in an urban setting with a very different climate than that of the Plains—and she was separated from her family and friends. Ask students to think of a time when they arrived at a new place—it could be a new home, a new school, or even visiting someone's home for the first time—and write about how they felt when they first got there. You may also wish to have students extend their writing to consider how they would treat someone who was coming to visit them for the first time. Where would they take their visitors? How would they respond to their guest's homesickness? What would they do to make the visit as comfortable as possible?

Be sure to give students opportunities to share their writing via read-alouds, bulletin boards, writing walls, learning centers, and so on.

Report About It

☆ **NATIVE AMERICANS TODAY:** In addition to being a doctor, Susan Picotte was a leading force in the community. Encourage students to research and report on contemporary Native American leaders, for example, Wilma Mankiller, Chief of the Cherokee nation; Ben Nighthorse Campbell, a United States Senator from Colorado; or Bill Yellowtail, a state senator in Montana. What are some of the concerns of Native Americans today? Also, ask students to find out how that person's tribal government is organized.

☆ **BEFORE AND AFTER MAPS:** Before 1854, Omaha lands covered almost 6 million acres, or about one-third of what is now Nebraska. After 1854, through the efforts of the U.S. government, the Omaha had only 300,000 acres on which to live. Invite students to focus on one Indian tribe and create before and after maps for that group. The first map should show the lands the tribe inhabited in the early 1800s and the second should show the lands inhabited by the end of the 1800s. At the bottom of the maps, students may list key events such as treaties and relocations. In addition to the Omaha, tribes who lost land or were forced to relocate in the 1800s include the Cheyenne, Sioux, Cherokee, Choctaw, and Seminole.

Nellie Bly
Investigative Reporter

≈≈≈

by Wendy Murray

Characters (in order of appearance):

NARRATORS 1-2
ELIZABETH COCHRANE/NELLIE BLY
MRS. COCHRANE: Nellie's mother
NEWSPAPER HAWKERS 1-3
PITTSBURGH RESIDENTS 1-10
FEMALE FACTORY WORKER 1
FEMALE FACTORY WORKERS 2-8 (nonspeaking roles)
FACTORY SUPERVISOR
WORLD REPORTER
OFFICE BOY
JOSEPH PULITZER
JOHN COCKERILL

ACT 1

★★★★★★ SCENE 1: 1885. A boarding house in Pittsburgh, Pennsylvania. Elizabeth Cochrane and her mother are sitting in their room.

NARRATOR 1: Welcome to Pittsburgh, Pennsylvania! Here and in other cities across the nation, more and more women are working outside the home. To put food on their tables they labor in mills, factories, offices, and kitchens.

NARRATOR 2: Meanwhile, many women who don't need to work for money are getting restless. They're tired of being told they are too delicate to work outside the home. They want equal rights with men. A movement led by Susan B. Anthony and Elizabeth Cady Stanton is demanding the vote for women.

NARRATOR 1: The idea of social change is making people nervous. Some women like being treated as delicate ladies. Many men think the idea of women's equality is ridiculous. Newspapers across the country debate the issue. In January of 1885, Erasmus Wilson, a writer for the *Pittsburgh Dispatch* publishes an article called "What Girls Are Good For."

NARRATOR 2: Mr. Wilson says women have no business working in shops and offices. Women should let their husbands take care of them. Little does he know that his words will launch the writing career of Elizabeth Cochrane—soon to be known as Nellie Bly!

ELIZABETH (throwing down the newspaper she has been reading): I've never been so angry in all my life! Who *is* this Erasmus Wilson? How can he say women shouldn't work when so many women have children to feed or elderly parents to take care of? They *have* to work, and there are hardly any jobs open to them. Not all women marry men who can take care of them—and not all want to! I'm going to write a letter to the newspaper.

MRS. COCHRANE: Oh, Elizabeth, it's such a beautiful day and we've been cooped up in this stuffy room for hours. Take a walk with me and get some fresh air. You can write your letter later.

ELIZABETH: No, Mother. I wouldn't enjoy the walk. I've got to speak my mind. I'll sign my letter "Lonely Orphan Girl" so the editor won't know for sure if I'm a woman, or a male writer disguising his identity. Maybe *then* he'll take the letter seriously!

(Elizabeth sits at her desk and begins to write a letter.)

ACT 2

SCENE: A busy street in Pittsburgh. Newspaper hawkers move about the stage selling copies of the *Pittsburgh Dispatch* to men and women passing by.

(The cast members onstage read the newspapers while the narrators speak.)

NARRATOR 1: Elizabeth Cochrane's angry letter to the *Dispatch* impressed the newspaper's editor, George Madden. Assuming it had been written by a man, Madden invited the "gentleman" writer to show him more of his work. Was he surprised when nineteen-year-old woman walked into his office!

NARRATOR 2: He was even more surprised when Elizabeth said she wanted to write an article on divorce. Divorce was a shocking subject in those days, but George Madden liked the boldness of Elizabeth's writing. He was a good businessman, too. He knew that controversy would sell newspapers.

NARRATOR 1: He gave Elizabeth the pen name Nellie Bly and told her to go ahead and write the article. When her article on "Mad Marriages" appeared in the paper, it caused a sensation.

NEWSPAPER HAWKERS 1-3: Extra! Extra! Read all about it! Get your copy of the *Dispatch* before they're all sold!

RESIDENT 1: Who's this Nellie Bly?

RESIDENT 2: It can't be a woman. Everyone knows women don't have logical minds. It must have been written by a man.

RESIDENT 3: If ladies write for newspapers, they should write about handkerchiefs, flower shows, recipes. *Not* divorce!

RESIDENT 4: The author must be a well-known feminist!

RESIDENT 5: Or a male writer hiding behind a *nom de plume.*

RESIDENT 6: A lady's name should appear in the newspaper only three times in her life—when she's born, when she marries, and when she dies.

RESIDENT 7: Would you look at that? Those newspapers are selling like hotcakes!

RESIDENT 8: Bravo to Nellie Bly, whoever she is! She's right! Divorce laws *are* unfair to women!

RESIDENT 9: Nellie Bly *has* to be a woman. She knows more about women than any man could know!

RESIDENT 10: It's better for a lady to say too little than too much.

ACT 3

★★★★★ **SCENE: A dimly lit room in a factory. The factory workers shiver. They have rags wrapped around their feet to protect them from the icy cement floor.**

NARRATOR 1 (speaking enthusiastically): Want a job in Pittsburgh? If you're an immigrant or an unskilled worker, we've got jobs for you! Come work in our iron and steel factories, or if you don't like that, we've got bottle factories galore! Why, Pittsburgh produces more champagne bottles than France!

NARRATOR 2 (turning to Narrator 1, arms crossed in disagreement): Yes, but none of those workers will *ever* earn enough to buy a bottle of champagne. They're so tired when they get home from working fourteen hours without a break that they fall into bed without supper. Who's looking out for them? Nellie Bly, that's who! Disguising herself as a poor woman, she works in a factory. Her articles on factory conditions are filled with the real details of the workers's lives. Nellie Bly's exposés help pave the way for child labor laws.

NELLIE (whispering to the woman working next to her): The light is so dim my head is beginning to ache!

FACTORY WORKER: We all have headaches. Don't talk to me or we'll get fined. They'll fine you for smiling.

FACTORY SUPERVISOR (pacing back and forth): Faster! Work faster! All of you!

NELLIE: I need a drink of water.

FACTORY SUPERVISOR: I've never seen a lazier bunch! What a bunch of good-for-nothings! Faster, I said! Work faster!

(Nellie walks away from the assembly line to get a drink of water.)

SUPERVISOR (turning to Nellie): Where do you think you're going?

NELLIE: I'm getting a drink of water. We haven't had anything to drink since—

SUPERVISOR: I don't care if it's been two years since you had a drink of water. You're fired!

NARRATOR 1: Nellie Bly didn't mind being fired—she had enough information for her story about how terribly the women workers were treated. When her article appeared in the newspaper, the factory owner was furious.

NARRATOR 2: That didn't stop Nellie Bly. She wrote about more factories. The owners got so mad they called the *Dispatch* and told George Madden they weren't going to advertise in the paper if Nellie Bly didn't stop making trouble.

ACT 4

★★★★★ SCENE: 1887. The newsroom of *The New York World* in New York City. Nellie Bly and an office boy stand outside Joseph Pulitzer's office.

NARRATOR 1: With factory owners and city officials threatening the newspaper, Nellie's boss George Madden decided it was best to let things calm down. He told Nellie to write about parties, art, and drama.

NARRATOR 2: Nellie put up with the assignment for a while, but then she got fed up with parties and art. She left for Mexico, where she wrote articles about the poverty she saw there. Her reports were published all over America.

NARRATOR 1: When Nellie returned to Pittsburgh, the city seemed dull. She quit her job and moved with her mother to New York City, where she was determined to get a job as a reporter for Joseph Pulitzer's *New York World*.

NARRATOR 2: In the summer of 1887, Nellie went to the *World* building in downtown Manhattan to see Mr. Pulitzer. She waited for more than three hours in the lobby.

OFFICE BOY: Mr. Pulitzer isn't receiving any visitors. Sorry, miss.

NELLIE: I'm not leaving until I see Mr. Pulitzer. Please let me through the gate.

***WORLD* REPORTER** (speaking to the office boy on his way into the office): What's going on here?

OFFICE BOY: This woman says she's a writer. She wants to see Mr. Pulitzer.

***WORLD* REPORTER** (laughing): Sorry, lady, we don't publish fluffy articles about flower arranging.

NELLIE: Good—because I don't write them!

(When the office boy isn't looking, Nellie dashes into Mr. Pulitzer's office. Pulitzer is sitting at his desk. Managing editor John Cockerill is seated in a chair in front of the desk.)

OFFICE BOY (running in to the office after Nellie): I'm sorry Mr. Pulitzer, she just ran right past me!

NELLIE (walking up to Pulitzer's desk and holding out her hand): Mr. Pulitzer, I'm sorry to disturb you. But I've been trying to see you for a long time. I'm Nellie Bly, recently of the *Pittsburgh Dispatch*. I brought some of my work to show you—

PULITZER: Miss Bly, did you run past my office boy here?

NELLIE: Well, sir, I guess I run faster than he does.

MR. PULITZER (bursting out laughing): Miss Bly, since you're here, you might as well

meet my managing editor, John Cockerill. Have a seat and show me your articles.

NARRATOR 1: After reading the articles, Joseph Pulitzer hired Nellie Bly. She wrote many articles about New York City's poor and ill people for the *New York World*. The articles made people stop and think.

NARRATOR 2: Nellie put herself in dangerous places to get a story. She went undercover in police stations, prisons, slums, and factories. In her most daring assignment, she pretended to be insane so she could report on the terrible treatment of patients inside a New York asylum.

NARRATOR 1: Nellie Bly became famous when she took a trip around the world in less than 80 days. Newspapers all over the world reported on her travels. It isn't only that globe-trotting journey for which Nellie Bly should be remembered.

NARRATOR 2: She should be celebrated for her many journeys closer to home—down the streets and into the factories where few writers had traveled. This was the work that was closest to Nellie's heart, for it was through these stories that she helped improve the quality of people's lives.

Nellie Bly
Teaching Guide

Elizabeth Cochrane, known as Nellie Bly, was born in Cochran Mills, Pennsylvania, on May 5, 1867. She was educated at home until 1879 and then attended school in Indiana, Pennsylvania. About 1881, Cochrane moved with her family to Pittsburgh. After writing a letter to the *Pittsburgh Dispatch* in response to an article on "What Girls Are Good For," its editor hired her as a reporter. She was dubbed Nellie Bly by *Dispatch* managing editor George A. Madden, who took one name from a popular song by Stephen Collins. Bly wrote a series of articles on the plight of working women that paved the way for more equitable labor laws—and made Pittsburgh factory owners furious. In 1886, Bly spent several months in Mexico, serving as a foreign correspondent for the *Dispatch*. In 1887, she joined the staff of the *New York World*. For one of her first assignments, Bly had herself committed to the insane asylum on Blackwell's Island in order to report on the deplorable conditions there. She also targeted corrupt politicians, callous police, and exploitive employers with her pen. In the fall of 1889, largely as a publicity stunt for the *World*, Bly went around the world in less than the 80 days it took Jules Verne's character, Phileas Fogg, to complete the journey. Her book about the trip—*Nellie Bly's Book: Around the World in 72 Days*—made her world famous and marked the peak of her career. She is the author of two other titles, *Six Months in Mexico* and *Ten Days in a Madhouse*. In 1895, Nellie married Robert Seaman, a wealthy Brooklyn manufacturer. When he died in 1904, she managed his Ironclad Manufacturing Company, saw it through an expensive litigation, and wound up broke. Between the years 1914 to 1919, Nellie Bly wrote for the *New York Evening Journal*. She died of pneumonia at the age of 57.

Book Links

A Biography of Nellie Bly: Making Headlines by Karen Lynn Emerson (Macmillan, 1989)

Nellie Bly: Journalist by Elizabeth Ehrlich (Chelsea House Publishers, 1989)

Nellie Bly: Reporter for the World by Martha E. Kendall (Millbrook, 1992)

EXTENSION ACTIVITIES

Talk About It

⭐ **CHARTING CHARACTERISTICS:** "I was too impatient to work along at the usual duties assigned women on newspapers," Nellie Bly said. Ask students what other characteristics, besides impatience, they think Nellie Bly possessed. Keep a running list of the characteristics on chart paper and hang it on the wall. Ask groups of students to come up with four or five qualities that a journalist probably *should* possess.

⭐ **EXPLORING THE REPORTER'S ROLE:** Nellie Bly visited men, women, and children in factories and slums, hospitals, and city streets. She talked to them about their lives and reported what she heard and saw. Why do you think she bothered to talk with people who were not rich and famous? What was she trying to do by publishing their stories in the newspaper? Do students believe that nowadays reporters can effect changes with their words? Ask them to give examples to back up their opinions.

Write About It

⭐ **DAY-IN-THE-LIFE STORIES:** Not all investigative reporters have to go undercover as Nellie Bly did. Invite students to investigate their own community or neighborhood and write a news article about it. They can write a "day in the life" story about the local supermarket, the movie theater, their parent's office, life on their street, and so on. Provide local, state, and national newspapers for students to study. Emphasize that investigative articles don't always have to focus on the negative. Many articles are human-interest pieces which spotlight a person or group in a community.

⭐ **REWRITE THE SONG:** George Madden took the name of Nellie Bly from a popular song of the time, written by Stephen Collins. If possible, provide the music for the lyrics below and share the song with the class. Ask students to rewrite the lyrics to *"Nellie Bly"* to describe the journalist Nellie Bly's career. Encourage them to give it a melody—or sing it to the tune of a well-known current song—and perform it for other classes.

> *Nelly Bly, Nelly Bly*
> *bring the broom along,*
> *We'll sweep the kitchen clear, my dear,*
> *and have a little song.*
> *Poke the wood, my lady love,*
> *and make the fire burn,*
> *And while I take the banjo down,*
> *just give the mush a turn.*
> *Heigh, Nelly, Ho, Nelly,*
> *listen love, to me;*
> *I'll sing for you, play for you,*
> *a dulcet melody.*

Be sure to give students opportunities to share their writing via read-alouds, bulletin boards, writing walls, learning centers, and so on.

Report About It

⭐ **FAVORITE FEMALE JOUNALISTS:** Which female journalists are the most influential in the 1990s? Let students choose a woman journalist in any medium—print, television, or radio—and analyze the types of stories she covers. If possible, have students bring in clippings, audiocassettes, or videotapes of the reporters's stories to punctuate their analyses. Also, ask students to present brief biographies of their subjects and explanations of why they chose particular journalists.

⭐ **TRACING BLY'S TRAVELS:** Where in the world did Nellie Bly go? How long did it take her? What kinds of transportation did she use? Today, what is the fastest amount of time in which a person could complete Nellie Bly's around-the-world trip? Have students prepare a detailed report of the places Nellie Bly visited and the length of time it took her to get from place to place. Then they should draw up a time table for a modern-day trip. Ask them to use a world map or globe to present their findings.

Orville and Wilbur Wright

First in the Air

by Timothy Nolan

Characters (in order of appearance):

NARRATOR
MAGGIE
MAGGIE'S MOTHER
ORVILLE WRIGHT
WILBUR WRIGHT
MR. AND MRS. WEBBER: Customers at the bicycle shop
OCTAVE CHANUTE: A famous engineer also working on an airplane
PHOTOGRAPHER

PROLOGUE

★ ★ ★ ★ ★ ★ ★ ★ SCENE: 1948. A small airport in Cincinnati, Ohio.

NARRATOR: Until the 1940s, most Americans traveled long distances by train. Then they began to realize that a faster, more comfortable way to travel around the country was available—the airplane. In a small airport in Cincinnati, Ohio, a young woman and her daughter are waiting for their flight. They don't realize that the older man standing near them is Orville Wright, who, with his brother Wilbur, made airplane flight possible.

MAGGIE: Mommy, how does the airplane stay in the sky?

MOTHER (nervously): I don't, know, Maggie, it just does.

MAGGIE: But why doesn't it fall down?

MOTHER: It just doesn't, Maggie. *Please*, don't ask me any more questions!

ORVILLE WRIGHT: It's the wings. The wings keep the airplane up in the air.

MOTHER: Excuse me?

ORVILLE WRIGHT: See the wings? See the part at the tips that go up and down? That's what makes the air move over the airplane. That's what keeps it in the air.

MAGGIE: Really?

ORVILLE WRIGHT: Sure. As long as there's air, the plane stays up.

MOTHER (relieved): Well, there's always air.

ORVILLE WRIGHT: Exactly.

MAGGIE: Gee, mister, how do you know so much about airplanes?

ORVILLE WRIGHT (smiling): Oh, I learned about them a long time ago.

ACT 1

★ ★ ★ ★ ★ ★ SCENE: Summer 1899. The Wright Brothers's bicycle shop in Dayton, Ohio. Orville Wright is in the front of the shop, helping two customers. Wilbur Wright sits in the back of the shop, reading.

ORVILLE: Oh, it's really not that difficult, Mr. Webber. Once you start, the force of your movement keeps you balanced.

MRS. WEBBER: See, Roger, I told you. I taught myself, Mr. Wright, but Roger won't let me go without him. So I'm trying to teach him.

ORVILLE: Really, Mr. Webber, riding a bicycle is as simple as walking down the street.

126

MR. WEBBER: Well, I won't do it—it's just not—

WILBUR (rushing over with the book)**:** Orville, take a look at this!

MR. WEBBER: It's just not natural. I've got two good legs and they can take me anywhere I want to—

ORVILLE: Yes, but a bicycle will make your legs stronger.

WILBUR: Orville, take a look at this page!

MRS. WEBBER: What have you got there, Wilbur?

WILBUR: A man in Germany—Otto Lilenthal, he's been working with gliders—he was able to fly with control! He was able to take off and turn some!

ORVILLE (taking the book)**:** Let me see that . . .

WILBUR (taking back the book)**:** Look—here's someone else—Octave Chanute. He's been doing experiments with wind resistance. He thinks it may be possible to build a machine that can fly! An airplane!

ORVILLE (pointing to a page in the book)**:** But look—he's not working the wings right. One good wind, and he's going to be in serious trouble.

MRS. WEBBER: A flying machine! How exciting! Just think . . . to be able to fly . . .

ORVILLE: If Chanute doesn't figure out a way to turn those wings, he could hurt himself.

WILBUR (snapping his fingers)**:** I've got it! Think of the way a bird flies. It doesn't flap its wings, it keeps them steady. But the wings move to the left or the right. That way it can bank from one side to the other. That's how a bird climbs and descends, too. The wings of an airplane have to do the same thing.

ORVILLE: I think you're right . . . with the right engine, and some way to work the wind . . . it could work!

WILBUR: There's that place in North Carolina I read about. The winds come right off the ocean—

MR. WEBBER: Hey—what about my bicycle?

ACT 2

★★★★★ SCENE: Late 1901. The Wright Brothers' workshop in Kitty Hawk, North Carolina. Wilbur is sitting at a workbench, looking over piles of notes. He looks depressed. A long wooden box is pushed under the workbench.

(Orville enters.)

ORVILLE: What's the matter?

WILBUR: I keep looking at these notes and all these figures. It *should* work, but everything we put up goes down with the first stiff wind. Maybe . . . maybe all those people in Dayton were right . . . maybe it just wasn't meant to happen.

ORVILLE: Remember what Dad used to say? If we weren't meant to fly, there wouldn't be a sky.

WILBUR: I don't know . . .

ORVILLE (taking a piece of paper off of Wilbur's desk): Take a look at this piece of paper. If I drop it— (he drops the piece of paper) it falls to the floor. If I put this same piece of paper in a wind, on one of our kites, it stays aloft. And it's heavier than air. Now if we could make a wind and design the right kind of wing, then we should have something that can carry an engine *and* a man.

WILBUR: *Make* a wind?

(Orville spies the wooden box underneath the workbench and pulls it out.)

ORVILLE: What if we built a wind tunnel?

WILBUR: A *what?*

ORVILLE: We take this box and put a fan at one end. There's our wind tunnel. Then we test the wings until we find the right one.

WILBUR: Do you think it'll work?

ORVILLE: There's only one way to find out.

ACT 3

★★★★★ SCENE 1: The Wright Brothers' workshop in Kitty Hawk, North Carolina.

NARRATOR: At their bicycle shop in Ohio, Orville and Wilbur had talked about Octave Chanute and his experiments with wind resistance. Chanute believed that it was possible to build a flying machine. The Wright Brothers knew of Chanute, but they never dreamed that Chanute knew who they were. Then one day they had a visitor.

CHANUTE (knocking on the door): Excuse me. I'm sorry to interrupt—

WILBUR: It can't be! It's Octave Chanute! I recognize him from his pictures!

CHANUTE: Ah! I have found you then. The Wright Brothers? Yes? I was told I could find you here. I've heard you're doing some experiments with flight.

WILBUR: We've based a lot of our work on what we read about your experiments.

CHANUTE: Could I see your figures?

WILBUR: Certainly.

(Wilbur stands aside and lets Chanute look over his papers. Chanute nods his head.)

CHANUTE: These are remarkable! I've never seen such thorough research. Where did you two study?

(Orville and Wilbur look at each other with uncertainty.)

ORVILLE: You mean college?

WILBUR: To be honest, Mr. Chanute, we never graduated from high school.

ORVILLE: We've just been reading—yourself, Lilenthal, Professor Langley—

CHANUTE: Lilenthal is dead. His glider crashed in a head wind.

ORVILLE: Oh no! That's terrible.

CHANUTE: He knew it was dangerous, but he was willing to take the chance.

ORVILLE: But you still believe that it's possible to build a flying machine, don't you?

CHANUTE: Yes, definitely. That's one of the reasons why I'm here. Have you had much success?

ORVILLE: We're doing some testing in a wind tunnel—

CHANUTE: A wind tunnel?

WILBUR: Here, come take a look at it. We're testing wing models until we find the one that's strong enough.

(Wilbur leads Chanute to the wind tunnel. Chanute studies the flow of wind when the fan is turned on.)

CHANUTE: And you designed this wind tunnel?

ORVILLE: Well . . . I guess we did.

CHANUTE: Remarkable. You realize . . . this could work.

ORVILLE: Do you really think so?

CHANUTE: Of course. I'm speaking to a gathering of engineers later in the month. I

think they'd like to meet both of you. I'd be honored if you would join me.

NARRATOR: Octave Chanute introduced Wilbur Wright to the Western Society of Engineers, while Orville remained in Kitty Hawk and worked with the wind tunnel. Soon the rest of the world began to hear about the Wright Brothers' work. It was slow going. After finding the right wing, the Wrights had to invent the propeller, since no one had ever used one before. Then came the problem with the engine.

SCENE 2: A year later. The Wrights' workshop in Kitty Hawk.

ORVILLE: Did you find the engine?

WILBUR (shaking his head)**:** It had the right horsepower, but it weighed four pounds. We need something about a pound and a half. Any word from Chanute?

ORVILLE (picking up a note off the desk and reading it)**:** Not good news. "Cannot locate engine. Looks like another challenge for you two. Good luck. Octave."

WILBUR: We figure out the wings, we get the propeller, and now—

ORVILLE: You know what? We're just going to have to build an engine ourselves.

WILBUR: Do you *know* how to build an engine?

ORVILLE: No, and I don't know anything about building an airplane, either, but we're doing that, aren't we?

NARRATOR: Wilbur and Orville built an engine that weighed almost two pounds. Although it was the lightest engine they could put together, it was still heavier than they would have liked it to be. Nevertheless, they put it in their airplane. On December 17, 1903, the Wright Brothers rolled their airplane *Flyer I* out of its hangar.

ACT 4
★★★★★★ **SCENE: December 17, 1903. Kill Devil Hill, near Kitty Hawk, North Carolina. Orville climbs into the Flyer I.**

WILBUR: You ready?

ORVILLE: Yeah.

WILBUR: Remember, the pedals control the back and forth. The carriage controls the wings. The handles control the climb and descend.

ORVILLE: Got it.

WILBUR: Orville?

ORVILLE: Yeah?

WILBUR: Good luck . . . and be careful, okay?

ORVILLE: Will do.

NARRATOR: Wilbur went to the back of the plane and turned the propeller. The engine kicked and then roared to life. Then he went in front and pulled the blocks away from the dolly on which the plane rested. The *Flyer I* rolled down the rail on the dolly. As it reached the end of the rail, Orville pulled back the handles as hard as he could. The *Flyer I* started to rise! It rose—one foot, two feet, three feet! It was flying! For 12 seconds, the airplane flew through the air! Orville brought the *Flyer I* to a soft landing on the North Carolina sand!

(Wilbur runs up to the plane. Orville climbs out.)

WILBUR: Are you all right?

ORVILLE: YIPPEE!!!

WILBUR: You're all right!

ORVILLE: You bet I am! Did you see? We got off the ground! Let's get it back on the dolly, I want to take it up again!

WILBUR: Oh, no, now it's my turn!

(The photographer runs up to Orville and Wilbur.)

PHOTOGRAPHER: Hey! Hey! You flew! You just flew that thing through the air! Wait till they see the pictures—

ORVILLE: You got a picture of the plane in the air?

PHOTOGRAPHER: Did I ever!

ORVILLE: Well, don't go anywhere. We're not finished flying yet.

(Orville and Wilbur go to the Flyer I and load it back on the dolly. When the plane is in place, Orville pats it on the wing.)

WILBUR: My turn?

ORVILLE: You bet it's your turn!

NARRATOR: The Wright Brothers flew four times that day. The longest flight lasted 59 seconds. As they built better and better airplanes, they began to sell them to the Army and to businessmen who wanted to fly people over long distances. By the 1930s, just 30 years later, the first airlines were born. Airplanes were used to help us win World War I and air combat became a mainstay in all wars after that. By the 1950s, passengers were flying in jets across the United States and across the oceans to other countries. The Wright Brothers's twelve seconds in the sky changed the world of transportation forever.

Wright Brothers
Teaching Guide

Wilbur Wright was born in 1867 in Indianapolis, Indiana, and Orville Wright was born three years later in Dayton, Ohio. Their father, a Pentecostal minister, served different areas, and the family moved frequently before settling in Dayton. The Wrights never had a lot of money and, as a result, the brothers left school and went to work at an early age. They loved to read, however, and read anything they could afford to buy or order. It was reading articles about Otto Lilenthal and Octave Chanute that first sparked their interest in building a flying machine. The Wright Brothers possessed remarkable engineering ability; they first built a printing press and printed their own newspaper and then they opened their bicycle shop in 1892. By 1895, they were designing and building their own bicycles and beginning their first experiments with kites. By 1901, they were trying different wings in a wind tunnel and also on gliders in Kitty Hawk, North Carolina. Their first flying machine took off in 1903, but it wasn't until 1908 that they were formally recognized as the inventors of the airplane. Wilbur died of typhoid in 1912, but Orville lived to see the airplane become one of the major forms of transportation in the world. He died in 1948.

Book Links

The Wright Brothers: Kings of the Air by Mervyn D. Kaufman (Chelsea House, 1993)

The Wright Brothers at Kitty Hawk by Donald J. Sobol (Scholastic, 1987)

First Flight: The Story of the Wright Brothers by Richard L. Taylor (Watts, 1990)

EXTENSION ACTIVITIES

Talk About It

⭐ **LET'S GO FLY:** Suppose the airplane had never been invented? Open a discussion about travel by asking students about their favorite trips. Where did they go? How did they get there? What made the trip so special? Provide a globe, maps, and atlases so students can show their destinations. Ask those who traveled by air how they could have gotten to their destinations by another means of transportation. Let those who traveled by land or water talk about how flying might have changed their trip. Compare and contrast the various means of transportation students have used. What are the advantages and disadvantages of each?

☆ **BRAINY BROTHERS:** In the play, Octave Chanute is surprised that the Wright Brothers never attended college. Just as airplane travel is more accessible to people today, so is a college education. Share the biographies of Orville and Wilbur Wright with the students. Ask them if the Wrights' lack of formal education surprised them as much as it did Chanute. What do students think accounted for the Wrights' success? Students may mention the brothers' reading, their engineering ability, their willingness to experiment, and/or their desire to learn. List their opinions on the chalkboard. After discussing each one, ask students which attribute they think is the most important. If the Wright Brothers were missing any of the attributes listed, do they think the brothers would have succeeded?

Write About It

☆ **GO ON A BIRD WATCH:** By watching how birds flew through the air, Wilbur Wright learned how the wings of an airplane should operate. Encourage students to watch birds in flight and record their impressions. How do birds use the air currents? How do they hold their wings? When do they flap their wings? How do they take off and land? Do different birds seem to have different patterns of flight? How does the flight of an airplane resemble that of a bird? Students may wish to use drawings to illustrate their observations.

☆ **IMAGINING KITTY HAWK:** A photographer captured the flight of the *Flyer I* on film. That perspective would have been different from Orville's in the cockpit and Wilbur's on the ground below. Talk about instances where the students have seen something that surprised or thrilled them, something that literally stopped them in their tracks. Then ask students to imagine that they were at Kitty Hawk that day. Set the stage by having them pretend that they don't know anything about the Wrights' experiment; they are walking along the beach when they see the *Flyer I* take off. Have them write a descriptive paragraph about what they saw and how they felt.

Be sure to give students opportunities to share their writing via read-alouds, bulletin boards, writing walls, learning centers, and so on.

Report About It

☆ **INVENT A VEHICLE:** Encourage students, in groups of four or five, to design and produce a model of a vehicle. Their research, like the Wrights's interest in Chanute's and Lilenthal's experiments, should provide a solid basis for their own inventions. Once they decide on whether to build a land-, air-, or sea-based vehicle, or a dual-purpose one, they should then assemble written and visual information about other similar vehicles. After the vehicles are completed, hold a transportation fair where the groups can promote their inventions.

Franklin Delano Roosevelt

The Man Who Never Gave Up

by Brian Black

Characters (in order of appearance):

JAMES ROOSEVELT: Franklin's father and narrator of play

RADIO ANNOUNCER

LOUIS HOWE: Newspaperman and political adviser

SARA ROOSEVELT: Franklin's mother

ELEANOR ROOSEVELT: Social crusader and First Lady

FRANKLIN DELANO ROOSEVELT: the 32nd President of the United States

ANNA:
JAMES:
ELLIOT: } Franklin and Eleanor's children
FRANKLIN, JR.:
JOHN:

ACT 1

★★★★★★ SCENE: 1920. Franklin and Eleanor Roosevelt's townhouse in New York City. Franklin, Eleanor, Sara, and Louis Howe are listening to the election returns on the radio.

JAMES ROOSEVELT: Cousin Teddy Roosevelt got his start in the New York State legislature, and that's where Franklin started, too. He was a Democrat, but he went into that Republican district, asking people for their votes. And he made it! State Senator Franklin Roosevelt! That was in 1910. In 1912, right after he was re-elected, President Woodrow Wilson called. "I want you to be my assistant secretary of the navy," he said. Franklin took the job. He took time off in 1914 to run for the United States Senator from New York. He lost. Now—the thing you have to know about my son Franklin is that he never gave up. In 1920, he was asked to run for vice president of the United States.

RADIO ANNOUNCER: The 1920 Presidential Election returns are final! Harding and Coolidge have won 61 percent of the vote! James Cox and Franklin Roosevelt have experienced one of the *worst* defeats in American history! The Roosevelt name didn't even do any good in New York—Franklin Roosevelt's home state!

LOUIS HOWE: It's only a minor setback. I told you that I'd make you President, and I will.

SARA: Maybe now you'll go back to being a lawyer. There's more wheeling and dealing on Wall Street than there is in Washington, D.C.

ELEANOR: The most important thing to remember about this election is that women voted for the first time. (teasing) I promise they'll *all* vote for you next time, Franklin.

FRANKLIN: You've turned into a first-rate campaigner, Eleanor. I wouldn't be surprised if you could deliver on that promise.

SARA: I don't want to hear anymore talk tonight about Franklin running for anything.

FRANKLIN: I saw a lot in those 32 states I visited during the campaign, Mother. I learned a lot from the people I talked to. Some of them don't have electricity in their homes. Some of them have worked all their lives, and once they've retired, they have no way to support themselves. We are the only industrial country in the world that doesn't provide security for our people. Workers who lose their jobs have no way to make ends meet until they find other jobs.

ELEANOR: Don't forget the children, Franklin, or their mothers.

FRANKLIN: I won't. You can be sure of that. I'll never forget seeing the tenement children you taught before we were married. I had never seen such poverty.

LOUIS HOWE (standing up to leave)**:** Well, I guess tomorrow morning's soon enough to start talking about the next race.

FRANKLIN: The moment of defeat is the best time to lay plan for future victories. Stay awhile, Louis.

ACT 2

★★★★★ **SCENE 1:** 1921. Campobello, the Roosevelt's island estate off the coast of Maine. Franklin, Eleanor, and their five children are on the front porch. Franklin sits in a chair while the others stand.

JAMES ROOSEVELT: This is the hard part for me to tell you about. Franklin grew up with every advantage I could give him. He'd traveled to Europe eight times— eight!—before he was fourteen years old. I was vice-president of the Delaware & Hudson Railroad. When we toured the United States, we used a private railroad car. But all that privilege couldn't protect him.

ELEANOR: A fire!

ANNA: Yes! It was huge!

JAMES: We were sailing by and I looked over and I saw smoke—

FRANKLIN, JR.: *I* looked over and *I* saw smoke—

ELLIOT: We *all* saw the smoke at the same time.

JOHN: I didn't see any smoke at all.

ANNA: We sailed over and we put it out!

ELEANOR: How in the world did you put it out?

ELLIOT: Evergreen branches!

FRANKLIN, JR.: I took my branches, and I beat that fire back—

JOHN: Look here—part of my eyebrow got burned off.

ELEANOR: My goodness! Let me take a look at all of you.

JAMES: We're fine. If we weren't fine, would we have gone swimming in the lagoon and then run for miles and miles—

ANNA: And *then* we dove right into the Bay of Fundy and went swimming again!

JOHN: It was freeeezing!

ANNA: Then we ran all the way back here, and here we are!

ELEANOR: Well, run inside and get cleaned up before dinner. (turning to Franklin)

136

And that includes you, Mr. Roosevelt. You're shivering. Go inside and have a hot bath before dinner.

FRANKLIN (rubbing his shoulder): I don't think I want dinner.

ELEANOR: Franklin, are you all right?

FRANKLIN: I've got a chill. I think I'll just go up and turn in.

(He rises with difficulty, as if his legs are sore. Worried, Eleanor helps him stand up and walk into the house.)

SCENE 2: The next morning. Franklin Roosevelt's bedroom at Campobello.

(Eleanor enters the bedroom. Franklin wakes up.)

ELEANOR: Good morning, sleepyhead. How are you feeling?

FRANKLIN (frowning): I've never felt so strange in my life.

(Eleanor feels Franklin's forehead.)

ELEANOR (concerned): You've got a fever. I'll go call the doctor right now.

FRANKLIN (impatiently): I'm sure it's just a cold. (He throws the covers aside.) I'll be fine once I've had breakfast.

(As he tries to put his weight on his left leg, it buckles underneath him. He falls back on the bed.)

ELEANOR: Franklin, what is it?

FRANKLIN: My leg's numb. I can't feel anything in my leg.

JAMES ROOSEVELT: The paralysis spread to Franklin's other leg and then to his arms. He couldn't even hold a pen. Many doctors visited Campobello. One said Franklin had a cold—a bad cold, another said massage would make him feel better. A doctor from Boston finally found out what was wrong. Franklin had polio. In 1921, little was known about polio except that it could paralyze a person's arms, legs, or entire body—if it didn't kill you. There was no known treatment because nobody knew what caused the disease.

ACT 3
★★★★★ SCENE: 1924. A family is sitting around the radio in their living room.

JAMES ROOSEVELT: As I said before, my son never gave up. It took three years, but he began to walk again with the support of leg braces and crutches. He exercised until his upper body was powerful. With the encouragement of Eleanor and Louis Howe, he continued to be a force in politics. Eleanor increasingly became Franklin's eyes and ears as she traveled around the country and made speeches that put forth his ideas. Franklin's return to politics was complete in 1924. He was asked to speak at the Democratic National Convention in New York City.

RADIO ANNOUNCER: Roosevelt is slowly making his way down the aisle toward the podium. I believe everyone here is shocked—and moved—by the sight. The braces Roosevelt must wear make his legs stiff. His steps are slow and awkward. His sixteen-year-old son James supports one arm. A crutch is underneath Roosevelt's other arm.

WOMAN: That poor man.

MAN: He's lucky to be alive.

RADIO ANNOUNCER: They have reached the platform. James Roosevelt now leaves his father . . . a hush has fallen over Madison Square Garden, ladies and gentlemen. With two crutches now supporting his entire weight. Franklin Roosevelt—diagnosed just three years ago with polio—makes his way to the podium. He grasps the podium with both hands. The crutches fall away! There's the famous Roosevelt smile! (shouting over the roar and applause of the crowd) He is back! Ladies and gentlemen, Franklin Roosevelt has returned to politics!

WOMAN: Think how hard he's had to work. He's had to learn to walk all over again. I'd vote for him. He knows what trouble is.

MAN: You can't vote for somebody because you feel sorry for him.

WOMAN: But that's just it—he doesn't let you feel sorry for him. Listen.

VOICE OF FRANKLIN ROOSEVELT: I ask you in all seriousness . . . to keep first in your hearts and minds the words of Abraham Lincoln—"With malice toward none, and charity for all."

ACT 4
★ ★ ★ ★ ★ ★ **SCENE: 1928. Warm Springs, Georgia.**

JAMES ROOSEVELT: Franklin first came to Warm Springs in 1924. People with polio exercised in the hot springs that were filled with minerals. After exercising in the water for several hours every day, Franklin was able to move his right leg. For the first time in three years, he was able to move his right leg! In 1926, he bought the rundown hotel at Warm Springs and turned it into a center for the treatment and study of infantile paralysis. Children from all the world were treated at the center. The next year, 1927, the Georgia Warm Springs Foundation was created. I'm sorry to say that the warm springs didn't cure my son's paralysis—or even improve move-

ment in his legs that much—but what he did there improved other people's lives. Anyway, Franklin returned to Warm Springs after the Democratic Convention. Party leaders wrote, telegraphed, and called him every day.

FRANKLIN: The party wants me to run for Governor of New York.

ELEANOR: The doctors say you could be walking in another two years if you stayed here and concentrated on your exercises.

LOUIS: That would set you up to run for governor in 1932—as a walking candidate. Then you're in position for the presidency in 1936. You've always said that you believed a president had to be able to walk.

FRANKLIN: The Democrats need a strong candidate in New York. Judging by the number of letters and phone calls I've gotten, they seem to think I can do it.

ELEANOR: Franklin, you may be able to walk soon without braces or crutches. Why not put off the governor's race for another four years?

FRANKLIN: If the Democrats don't have a strong governor in New York, we won't be able to put Smith in the White House. It'll go to the Republicans.

LOUIS: I'm telling you right now that Smith can't win. If he loses, so do you. Wait four years. What's the big deal?

FRANKLIN: The Democratic Party needs me now.

ELEANOR: It sounds as if you've made up your mind.

FRANKLIN: I have.

JAMES ROOSEVELT: On January 1, 1929, Franklin became governor of New York. Later that year, the stock market crashed, sending the country into the Great Depression. In 1932, the American people overwhelmingly voted for Franklin as President of the United States. Though he was physically handicapped, no one ever doubted that my son was a man of action. In his inauguration speech, Franklin told the American people that "the only thing we have to fear is fear itself." Those weren't just words. That's the way he lived his life.

Franklin Delano Roosevelt
Teaching Guide

Franklin Delano Roosevelt was born into a world of privilege on January 30, 1882, at the family estate near Hyde Park, New York. His father, James, was the vice-president of the Delaware & Hudson Railroad. His mother, Sara Delano, was James' second wife. James died while Franklin was a freshman at Harvard. Childhood friends and fifth cousins, Franklin and Eleanor Roosevelt were married in 1905. Eleanor was given away by her uncle, Theodore Roosevelt, who was President of the United States at the time. Franklin and Theodore were also distant cousins, and Franklin followed in the political footsteps of Teddy. Despite being struck by polio in 1921, Franklin Roosevelt continued his involvement in politics. He was elected governor of New York State in 1928 and President in 1932. He presided over some of the most troubled times in American history. Always calm under pressure, Roosevelt presented Americans with his recovery plan, the New Deal. He was also President on December 7, 1941, when Pearl Harbor was attacked by the Japanese, pulling the U.S. into World War II. On April 12, 1945, during an unprecedented fourth term, Franklin Roosevelt died in office.

Book Links

Franklin Delano Roosevelt by Russell Freedman (Clarion Books, 1990)

The Franklin Roosevelts by Cass R. Sandak (Macmillan, 1992)

Franklin D. Roosevelt and the New Deal by Sharon Shebar (Barron, 1987)

EXTENSION ACTIVITIES

Talk About It

⭐ **REMEMBERING RADIO DAYS:** Before the advent of television, radios were the primary sources of news and entertainment in homes across America. Invite several people who listened to Roosevelt's Fireside Chats on the radio when they were growing up to speak to your class. Before the guests arrive, hold a brainstorming session with students to come up with questions they'd like to ask. Also encourage them to formulate new questions as the speakers share their stories.

⭐ **PUBLIC HEALTH PROGRESS:** Thanks to a vaccine, polio is no longer the dreaded disease that it was in Roosevelt's time. Share your own memories about polio and what kind of vaccine you received against the disease. Then ask students to talk about their own vaccinations.

Write About It

⭐ **1941 DIARIES:** One of Franklin Roosevelt's most dramatic speeches was when he told the American people that Pearl Harbor had been bombed. Locate a recording of that speech. As you play the speech, invite students to pretend they are in their homes in 1941, listening to their radios. Afterward, ask them to write a diary entry about the experience. How did the news make them feel? Did Roosevelt's words and voice soothe them and give them confidence? Did they think he would be able to handle the crisis effectively?

Be sure to give students opportunities to share their writing via read-alouds, bulletin boards, writing walls, learning centers, and so on.

Report About It

⭐ **EXTRAORDINARY ELEANOR:** Eleanor Roosevelt was an outspoken First Lady. She had many causes that she championed. Have students prepare biographies about Eleanor Roosevelt in which they also discuss how she changed the role of the First Lady. Ask them to conclude with their own opinions about Eleanor Roosevelt.

⭐ **THE NEW DEAL IN THE 90'S:** Roosevelt's New Deal affected every corner of the country. Chances are there is a WPA mural in your local post office or a park in your neighborhood that the CCC built. Encourage students to play detective and uncover how FDR's New Deal programs are still visible in your community today.

⭐ **ROOSEVELT RIVALRY:** Franklin Roosevelt's political career mirrored his cousin Teddy Roosevelt's. After students research both men's careers, have them compare and contrast the two. Ask them to include in their reports which man they think was the better president and why they think so.

Amelia Earhart
Flying into the Unknown

by Jacqueline Charlesworth

Characters (in order of appearance):

NARRATOR
BOBBY: Playmate of Amelia and Muriel Earhart
MURIEL EARHART: Amelia's younger sister
AMELIA EARHART
SAM: A playmate of Amelia and Muriel
GRANDMOTHER OTIS: Amelia and Muriel's grandmother
GRANDFATHER OTIS: Amelia and Muriel's grandfather
MARION PERKINS: Head of the community center
where Amelia was a social worker
HILTON RAILEY: Promoter of early flying stunts
FRANKLIN D. ROOSEVELT: President of the United States
ELEANOR ROOSEVELT: First Lady of the United States
FEMALE DINNER GUESTS 1-2
COMMANDER WARNER THOMPSON OF THE U.S. COAST
GUARD
COAST GUARD RADIO OPERATOR

ACT 1

★★★★★ SCENE: Early 1900s. Late in the afternoon on a spring day. Amelia's grandparents are sitting in chairs on the front porch of a large wooden house in Atchison, Kansas. A group of children, including Amelia and Muriel, can be heard playing offstage.

NARRATOR: In the early part of the 1900s, the idea of flying was a new one—at least for human beings. Airplanes had only recently been invented and were not nearly as safe as they are today. It was up to a few courageous individuals—people who were willing to try out the new machines—to get flying off the ground.

(A loud discussion among the children can be heard coming from behind the house.)

BOBBY: I want to go first! I want to go first!

MURIEL: Oh, Amelia, let me go! I helped make it!

AMELIA: *I'm* the one who dreamt it up, so I should be the guinea pig. Don't worry—as long as I don't crash, you'll all get a turn!

SAM: There she goes!

MURIEL AND BOBBY: Yaaaay!

GRANDFATHER OTIS (to Grandmother Otis): What do you suppose they're up to now?

GRANDMOTHER OTIS: Honestly, those girls are just too wild. Imagine running around in trousers and playing like that with boys! Their mother needs to teach them how to behave like proper young ladies. You'd think we didn't raise her right. When she comes over to pick them up, I'm going to have a talk with her.

AMELIA: Whooooeee! It's just like flying! Wheeeeeee!

(A loud rattling noise is heard, accompanied by much laughter and shouting.)

GRANDMOTHER OTIS (rising from her seat and walking toward the side of the house): Well that does it! (shouting) Ameliaaah!! Muuriel! You girls come here this instant!

(Amelia and Muriel come running around the corner of the house, breathless and disheveled.)

GRANDMOTHER OTIS: What was all that noise?

MURIEL: Oh, Grandma, it was so exciting! Amelia built a roller coaster on top of the old shed!

GRANDFATHER OTIS: A what?

AMELIA: A roller coaster, Grandpa. I nailed some fence rails going down one side of the roof to make a track, and then I took the wheels from my old roller skates and attached them to a plank to make a cart. Then—

GRANDMOTHER OTIS: That's enough! There will be no roller coasters in my backyard! My word! Why can't you two play in a ladylike fashion? Why, when I was a girl, the most daring thing I ever did was roll my hoop in the town square. You go inside this very minute and clean up for supper. Go on now!

AMELIA AND MURIEL (reluctantly): Yes, Grandma.

(The girls climb the porch steps and enter the house.)

GRANDFATHER OTIS (with pride): That Amelia! I wonder what she'll be like when she grows up.

ACT 2

★★★★★★ SCENE: April 1928. A community center in Medford, Massachusetts.

NARRATOR: As she grew older, Amelia didn't lose interest in daredevil activities. After she left college, she took flying lessons. By the time she was 25, Amelia had her pilot's license. Even though she loved it, flying was still just a hobby. Amelia took a job as a social worker in a town near Boston, Massachusetts, where she helped immigrants adjust to life in America. One day Amelia received a telephone call that changed her life forever.

MARION PERKINS (calling down the hall): Amelia! You have a telephone call.

AMELIA (entering office): Thanks, Marion. (into telephone) This is Amelia Earhart.

HILTON RAILEY (from offstage): Miss Earhart, allow me to introduce myself. My name is Hilton Railey. I'm involved in a very exciting project, and I thought we might work together on it. I understand you're interested in flying?

AMELIA: I'm not interested in it—I love it.

HILTON: Miss Earhart, would you be willing to do something important for the cause of aviation?

AMELIA: Such as?

HILTON: Such as flying a plane across the Atlantic Ocean. No other woman's pulled it off. You'd be the first.

AMELIA: Mr. Railey, I should tell you that when a great adventure is offered, I don't refuse it!

144

NARRATOR: In June 1928, Amelia, flying with two male pilots, became the first woman to cross the Atlantic by plane. She was immediately hailed as a great hero by women and men all around the world. Her career as an aviator had taken off.

ACT 3

★★★★★ **SCENE: 1933. A formal dinner at the White House. President Franklin D. Roosevelt is seated at the head of a long table of guests. His wife Eleanor sits a few seats away, beside Amelia.**

NARRATOR: After flying with two copilots across the Atlantic, Amelia decided that she should try the flight alone. On May 19, 1932, she took off from Newfoundland, Canada. It was a difficult voyage. Her altimeter, the instrument which shows how high the plane is flying, broke early in the trip. Also, for much of the flight, flames were shooting out of a crack near the engine. Fifteen hours and eighteen minutes after takeoff, Amelia made world headlines when she landed her small plane in a meadow in Ireland. That day, the President and the First Lady, like many others, became Earhart's admirers.

ELEANOR ROOSEVELT: Amelia, what will your next adventure be?

FEMALE DINNER GUEST 1: Yes, do tell us!

AMELIA: Well . . . no one's ever flown from California to Hawaii . . . or perhaps I'll take a crack at flying around the world.

FEMALE DINNER GUEST 2: Miss Earhart, if I may say so, you are truly an inspiration to women. Your daring is a credit to us all.

FRANKLIN ROOSEVELT: I agree! You've proven that there's nothing a woman can't do once she puts her mind to it.

AMELIA (modestly)**:** I think the most important thing is to follow one's ambitions. I shall be quite happy if I contribute in even a small way to the advancement of women.

FRANKLIN: Well, you've inspired my wife for one. She wants to take flying lessons!

ELEANOR: Yes, I confess I do. I'm terribly fond of flying. Why, I would go for an airplane ride right now if someone offered one.

AMELIA: Then let's go! There's nothing like a short hop at night.

FEMALE DINNER GUEST 2 (shocked)**:** In your evening gowns?!

ELEANOR: What better way? Excuse us, ladies and gentlemen.

AMELIA: Save some dessert for us.

(Amelia and Eleanor Roosevelt leave the dining room.)

ACT 4

SCENE: July 3, 1937. Early morning in the radio room of the American ship *Itasca* in sight of a small island in the Pacific Ocean. Commander Thompson and the radio operator are listening to the radio.

NARRATOR: On June 1, 1937, Amelia took off from Florida on the first leg of an around-the-world journey. She was accompanied by Fred Noonan, her navigator. By early July, they had landed in Puerto Rico, Brazil, Senegal, India, Indonesia, Australia, and New Guinea. From New Guinea, Amelia was to fly to Howland Island, a tiny island in the Pacific Ocean. Then she was to go on to Hawaii and California. The U.S. ship *Itasca* was waiting near Howland Island to guide Amelia's plane to the island. The following dialogue is based on the actual radio transmissions between Amelia and the *Itasca*.

COMMANDER THOMPSON (to radio operator): Have we heard anything from Earhart yet?

RADIO OPERATOR: Not yet sir. Wait—I seem to be picking up something.

AMELIA (her voice can be heard only faintly over the static of the radio): KHAQQ . . . weather cloudy . . . weather cloudy.

RADIO OPERATOR: What is your position? When do you expect to arrive at Howland?

NARRATOR: There is no response.

RADIO OPERATOR: What is your position? Your position, please!

NARRATOR: There is still no response. Commander Thompson goes on deck and scans the skies. Earhart's plane is nowhere to be seen. He returns to the radio room. Some time later, the *Itasca* picks up another signal.

AMELIA: I need a bearing. Please tell me what my position is.

RADIO OPERATOR: We are trying—wait, we are losing your signal—Hello! Hello!

NARRATOR: The signal is gone. The radio operator looks at Commander Thompson and shakes his head. There is still no visual sighting of Amelia Earhart's plane. Time passes . . . and then . . . there is one more transmission.

AMELIA: We must be on you but cannot see you. Gas is running low. Have been unable to reach you by radio. We are flying at 1,000 feet—

NARRATOR: Amelia's voice is lost again. Commander Thompson leans close to the radio . . .

AMELIA: We are on the line of position 157-337. We are running north and south.

COMMANDER THOMPSON: Now what could that mean? She must be nearly out of gas!

RADIO OPERATOR: I've lost her again! Hello! Hello! Please come in! Please come in!

NARRATOR: Amelia Earhart's voice was never heard again. The United States government conducted a massive search, but her plane was never found. There are many theories about Earhart's disappearance; most experts believe her plane ran out of fuel and sank in the Pacific Ocean somewhere near Howland Island. There is one thing we do know for sure: Amelia Earhart wasn't afraid to follow her dreams.

Amelia Earhart
Teaching Guide

Amelia Mary Earhart was born in Atchison, Kansas, on July 24, 1897. In 1916, she entered the Ogontz School, a two-year women's college near Philadelphia. During a 1917 visit to her sister Muriel in Toronto, Amelia was horrified to see the wounded soldiers returning from World War I. Rather than finish her studies at Ogontz, she decided to work as a nurse's aide in a Toronto hospital. Through her work she befriended a number of British and French pilots whose stories sparked her desire to fly. After the war, Amelia moved to California, where her parents were then living, and began taking flying lessons. In 1922, she received her pilot's license and in that same year set a women's altitude record at a Los Angeles air show. In 1924, she relocated to Medford, Massachusetts, and took a job as a social worker at Denison House, a settlement house serving the immigrant community. Flight promoter Hilton Railey asked Earhart if she would consider flying with two male pilots across the Atlantic. Amelia agreed; on June 18, 1928, she became an instant celebrity when she landed in Ireland. In 1931, Amelia Earhart married George Putnam, her manager. Her most spectacular flight was probably her transatlantic solo in 1932, which was beset by problems. She became the first person to fly from Hawaii to California and in that same year, 1935, the first person to solo from California to Mexico City. Two years later, on July 3, 1937, during an around-the-world flight, Amelia Earhart lost contact with ground-support crews while traveling from New Guinea to Howland Island in the Pacific Ocean. Her plane has never been found.

Book Links

Amelia Earhart: Courage in the Sky by Mona Kerby (Puffin Books, 1990)

Lost Star: The Story of Amelia Earhart by Patricia Lauber (Scholastic, 1988)

Amelia Earhart: Adventure in the Sky by Francesca Sabin (Troll Associates, 1983)

Amelia Earhart: Aviator by Nancy Shore (Chelsea House Publishers, 1987)

EXTENSION ACTIVITIES

Talk About It

☆ **OTHER GROUNDBREAKING WOMEN:** Amelia was a hero for women of her time. Ask students to explain why they think she was so influential. Have them contribute the names of other women who are famous for succeeding in positions or fields that traditionally have been closed to females. Then let them give examples of positions and fields that they feel are still male-dominated. What do students think the reasons are? Do they expect the situation to change?

Write About It

⭐ **SOLVING THE MYSTERY:** The question of Amelia Earhart's ultimate fate is still a mystery. While most researchers believe she ran out of fuel and crashed in the Pacific Ocean, there are those who think she and Fred Noonan may have made it to another island where they lived for a time. Still others are convinced that Earhart was on a secret spy mission for the United States and was captured by enemy forces. Another theory has it that she ended up living in New Jersey as a housewife under an assumed name! After reviewing these theories with the class, ask students to write a fifth act for the play in which they develop an idea of their own. The story line can be either based on one of the above theories or strictly imaginary. Students may wish to include navigator Fred Noonan as a character.

⭐ **JOURNEY LOGS:** Earhart kept logs of her journeys in which she recorded her observations about the weather, scenery, and people she met. During her around-the-world journey, she mailed copies of her log entries back to the United States so they could be published in a newspaper and people could follow her progress. If possible, locate copies of these logs and share them with the class. Then have students keep their own logs for a weekend, making entries five or six times a day. They may record information about the weather, what they ate, where they went, and who and what they saw. On Monday invite students to share their logs with the rest of the class.

Be sure to give students opportunities to share their writing via read-alouds, bulletin boards, writing walls, learning centers, and so on.

Report About It

⭐ **TRAVEL MAPS:** To give students a sense of the enormity of Earhart's final journey, have them research the exact route of her around-the-world trip. Using a flat map of the world, mark the places she visited with dots and connect them with solid lines. Mark the places she was to visit with hollow circles, drawing dotted lines to those destinations. For each place visited, ask students or group of students to report on what Amelia might have found there: the climate, the landscape, the peoples and their cultures.

⭐ **PHOTO-FILLED TIMELINES:** What else was going on in the world when Amelia was thrilling the public with her flying stunts? Have students collaborate to create a time line from 1920 through 1941 illustrating key events and trends of that era. Students may draw or find pictures representing women's suffrage, Prohibition, flappers, Charles Lindbergh, Hollywood movie stars, the stock-market crash, the Great Depression, the election of Franklin D. Roosevelt, the rise of Hitler, the beginning of World War II in Europe, the United States's entry into the war, and so forth, and paste

them at the appropriate points along the line. Underneath each picture they should include a brief explanation of the event or trend. After the time line is completed, invite the class to draw connections between Amelia's achievements and popularity and the events of her time. How are people's lives shaped by history and vice versa?

★ **WOMEN AVIATORS:** While Amelia Earhart is one of the world's most famous female aviators, other women have made their mark in the sky. Suggest that students find out about other women who have loved to fly, such as Jacqueline Cochran, Beryl Markham, Sally Ride, Jeana Yeager, and Janet H. Bragg. They may also wish to research the role of women pilots in the military, such as, the Women Air Service Pilots (Wasps) during World War II.

Langston Hughes
Finding the Words

by Helen H. Moore

Characters (in order of appearance):

NARRATORS 1-2
LANGSTON HUGHES: Ages 6, 16, and adult
JAMES HUGHES: Langston's father
CARRIE HUGHES: Langston's mother
READERS 1-2

ACT 1

★★★★★ **SCENE 1:** *Summer of 1908. James Hughes' house in Mexico City.*

NARRATOR 1: Langston Hughes was born in Joplin, Missouri, in 1902. During the course of his life, he lived in many places—Paris, France; Moscow, Russia; and Harlem in New York City. He's celebrated and beloved for his poetry, his stories, and his plays.

NARRATOR 2: In the beginning, Langston Hughes's life was difficult. His father James Hughes had studied the law and wanted to be a lawyer. He couldn't fulfill his dreams because the state of Missouri wouldn't let African Americans take the law exam. Hoping to escape discrimination, James moved to Mexico shortly after his son was born. His wife Carrie refused to go. She and Langston stayed behind in Missouri.

NARRATOR 1: When Langston was six years old, James Hughes sent a letter to Carrie, asking her and Langston to come and live with him in Mexico. Carrie decided to give it a try.

CARRIE: James, you've done so well for yourself. Practicing law . . . buying property . . . I'm so proud of you.

JAMES: You know I've never been afraid of hard work. As long as white people don't shut me out, I do fine.

CARRIE: Things are changing in the states, James. Langston's sure to have it better than we did.

JAMES: Don't count on it.

CARRIE: Oh, James, is it really so much better here in Mexico? I don't understand a word they're saying.

JAMES: Take a look at me. Take a good look. I'm a success here in Mexico. Why would I want to go back up there? You and Langston will have a good life here with me. I've got my eye on a ranch a couple of hours from here. When the time comes, I'll send Langston to college so he can learn how to run a modern ranch.

CARRIE: James! He's only six years old! Maybe he won't want to run a ranch. What's right for you may not be right for him. (She stops suddenly.) Oh! What was that?

JAMES: Get in the doorway! Hurry up!

LANGSTON: Mama!

NARRATOR 2: They heard a loud, rumbling sound under their feet. The floor pitched—the whole house shook. Dishes flew out of the cupboards. Pictures fell off the walls. The walls cracked open. Tarantulas, large hairy spiders, scrambled out of

152

the cracks. Carrie grabbed Langston and ran outside. James ran after them.

CARRIE: What *was* that? What was it?

JAMES: An earthquake. We've had worse. You all come back inside. Hurry up!

CARRIE: We're not going back into that house!

JAMES: Now, Carrie, those spiders aren't poisonous. They may not be pretty, but they won't hurt you.

LANGSTON: Mama! I want to go home! I'm afraid!

CARRIE: Go get our bags, James. We're leaving.

SCENE 2: Summer of 1919. Cleveland, Ohio.

NARRATOR 1: Carrie and Langston moved back to the United States, but James insisted on staying in Mexico. Back in the states, times were hard. Carrie Hughes was sometimes unable to find a job. There were times when she and Langston had little to eat. The Hughes divorced, and Carrie remarried. That marriage, unfortunately, didn't last.

NARRATOR 2: Carrie Hughes loved to read, and she passed that love on to her son. Langston wrote his first poem in honor of his graduation from school. Other poems followed.

NARRATOR 1: Langston didn't see his father again until he was 17 years old. At the end of his junior year in high school, James Hughes wrote his son, inviting him to spend the summer with him. His mother didn't want him to go.

LANGSTON: Why don't you want me to go to Mexico?

CARRIE: You might not want to come back.

LANGSTON (laughing): Don't worry, Ma. I still remember that earthquake and all those spiders pouring out of the walls!

CARRIE: Ooohh, don't remind me!

LANGSTON (still laughing): I'm sorry, Ma. Really, I'm sorry.

CARRIE (playfully angry): Oh, you are not! I'll never forget that day as long as I live!

LANGSTON (turning serious): I do feel a little nervous. I don't remember much about my father. I just remember that he seemed angry all the time. I don't understand why he moved to Mexico, away from us.

CARRIE: He couldn't make a living here in the states, Lang. No one here would hire a black lawyer. He had a chance in Mexico.

LANGSTON: But why is he still so mad?

CARRIE: You remember last summer vacation, when you went looking for a job?

LANGSTON (with anger): I'll never forget!

CARRIE: Your white friends got jobs right away, but nobody would hire you. You look like you're still pretty angry about that.

LANGSTON (slowly nodding his head): I am. At least I know I've got a job this summer. Maybe I'll make a good cowboy.

CARRIE: Just make sure you come back—and, Lang? Just make sure you don't come back angry.

ACT 2
★★★★★ **SCENE 1: Summer of 1919. James Hughes' house in Toluca, outside of Mexico City.**

NARRATOR 1: Langston did go to Mexico that summer. James Hughes was glad to see his son, but he was away most of the day on business. Before he left, he would give Langston several bookkeeping problems to solve that day. Langston was lonely, but he became friends with Maximiliano, a Mexican boy who took care of the horses. James Hughes had something to say about the friendship.

JAMES: Langston, why are you wasting your time with that Mexican? He'll never amount to anything. And he's certainly not a suitable friend for the son of a businessman like me.

LANGSTON: Maximiliano's a good friend! I'd have died of loneliness if it weren't for him! He's taught me how to take care of the horses. Shouldn't a rancher's son know how to do that?

JAMES: I don't want you going to his house anymore. People judge you by the company you keep.

LANGSTON: I don't care! We have a lot to talk about! I don't care what color a person's skin is, or where they live, or what they do! I judge people by the way they act, by the kind of person they are!

JAMES: Those are nothing but fancy words. You'll find that out soon enough. Skin color might not be important to you, but it sure is important to the rest of the world. I'd have been an important lawyer back in the states if not for the color of my skin. Don't tell me skin color isn't important!

LANGSTON: Dad, I can't deny that some people *are* prejudiced. You weren't treated right and that's unfair. That doesn't mean that *I* have to be prejudiced, too! I like *all* kinds of people.

154

JAMES: Have you finished the problems I gave you this morning?

LANGSTON: Not all of them—

JAMES: Why not? Go finish them right now. Hurry up!

NARRATOR 2: Langston loved his father. He saw how much his father had been hurt by his experiences. Unfortunately, James Hughes couldn't see how his behavior hurt and confused his son. The day Langston was due to travel to his father's ranch, he fell ill with a stomach infection. He returned to the United States soon afterward.

SCENE 2: Summer of 1920. Train station in Cleveland, Ohio.

NARRATOR 1: When he graduated from high school the next year, Langston wanted to go to college. He had been elected class poet in high school, and he wanted to be a writer. Carrie couldn't afford to send him. Once again, James Hughes invited his son to spend the summer working on his ranch in Mexico. It seemed like a good solution. Langston could earn some of the money for college by working at the ranch. His father might lend or give him the rest.

CARRIE: Lang, I wish I could afford to send you to college myself. I know how hard it is for you to ask your father for help.

LANGSTON: I don't mind working on the ranch to earn money. It'll give me something to write about!

CARRIE (wiping away a tear): I'll miss you, son. Now go on, get on board before you miss the train.

LANGSTON (boarding the train): I'll miss you, too.

NARRATOR: As the train made its way south and west, Langston listened to the rhythm of the great metal wheels chugging along the tracks. The metal seemed to sing, and the gentle rocking was like a slow dance. The gentle motion made Langston think of his mother and grandmother, and how much he loved them. He thought of his father, and the prejudice he and other African Americans had suffered, and felt sad. As the train crossed over the Mississippi River near St. Louis on its way to Mexico, Langston thought of the strength of the black people he had known, a strength that reached all the way back to Africa. He looked down at the muddy river and connected its strength with that of his ancestors.

(Langston writes down the poem as the readers on stage read it.)

READER 1:
I've known rivers:

I've known rivers ancient as the world and older than the flow of human blood in human veins.

My soul has grown deep like the rivers.

READER 2:

I bathed in the Euphrates when dawns were young.

I built my hut near the Congo and it lulled me to sleep.

I looked upon the Nile and raised the pyramids above it.

I heard the singing of the Mississippi when Abe Lincoln
    went down to New Orleans, and I've seen its muddy
    bosom turn all golden in the sunset.

READERS 1 AND 2 TOGETHER:

I've known rivers:

Ancient, dusky rivers.

My soul has grown deep like the rivers.

ACT 3
★ ★ ★ ★ ★ **SCENE: Summer of 1920. James Hughes' house in Toluca, Mexico.**

NARRATOR 1: As soon as he got to Mexico, Langston found a mailbox and sent his poem to *The Crisis*, a magazine founded by scholar and writer W.E.B. Du Bois and published in New York City. Then he got busy working on the ranch. Eventually, James Hughes did agree to pay Langston's way through college—but there was a catch.

JAMES: I'll pay for your education—as long as you study to become a mining engineer.

LANGSTON: An *engineer!* Dad, I don't want to be an engineer! I want to be a writer!

JAMES: Writing's a waste of time! Who'll publish this writing of yours? Give me an answer, hurry up!

LANGSTON: Someone will. I know they will.

NARRATOR 2: James Hughes planned to send Langston to college in Switzerland and then to Germany to an engineering school. Langston wrote furiously that summer: poems, articles, and a children's play. Then one day a copy of *The Crisis* arrived in the mail. Langston paged through it furiously. His poem "The Negro Speaks of Rivers" had been published!

LANGSTON (excitedly, waving the magazine back and forth): Dad—look! Look! My poem, it's been published!

JAMES: Let me see that.

(After he reads the poem, he looks at his son with respect.)

LANGSTON (shyly): What do you think?

JAMES: How much did this magazine pay you?

LANGSTON: It's my first published poem!

JAMES: Nothing, huh? Now don't let them take advantage of you. The money will come as you get experience. All right, I'll pay for you to go to college . . . to study writing.

LANGSTON: Really? You will? Thanks, Dad!

JAMES: Don't thank me. Just work hard and be a success.

NARRATOR 1: Langston *did* work hard. He is considered to be one of America's great poets. He wrote plays, short stories, and articles, as well as poems. Hughes also started theater companies all over the United States where young people could learn playwriting and performing. In all his works and words, Langston Hughes tried to portray the good in people of all races.

Langston Hughes
Teaching Guide

Langston Hughes was born in Joplin, Missouri, on February 1, 1902. Hughes worked as a deckhand, a dishwasher, and in a laundry, and the life of the average working black man and woman became the subject and theme of most of his writing. He eventually gained fame for his poems after poet Vachel Lindsay discovered him. Hughes had long admired Lindsay's poetry. While working as a busboy in a hotel in Washington, D.C., Hughes heard that the poet was staying at the hotel. That night, while Lindsay was eating dinner in the hotel, Langston stopped briefly at the poet's table, expressed his admiration for Lindsay's poems, and left some of his own. When Langston reported for work the next day, he was met at the entrance of the hotel by newspaper reporters and photographers who wanted to see the new poet that Vachel Lindsay had found. Soon Hughes' first book of poetry, *The Weary Blues* was published. After its publication, Hughes gained a patron and a scholarship to Lincoln University, where his classmates included Cab Calloway. Hughes traveled extensively; in 1936, he went to Spain and covered the civil war there for a newspaper. At the time of his death on May 22, 1967, he had produced a body of work that included not only poetry but also plays, articles, short stories, and a series of books based on a character named "Simple" who celebrated everyday life in Harlem.

Book Links

Langston Hughes, Young Black Poet by Montrew Dunham (The Bobbs-Merrill Company, Inc., 1972)

Langston Hughes by Jack Rummel (Chelsea House, 1989)

Langston Hughes, American Poet by Alice Walker (Thomas Y. Crowell Co., 1974)

EXTENSION ACTIVITIES

Talk About It

⭐ **EXPLORING A POEM:** In his poem "The Negro Speaks of Rivers," Langston Hughes makes a metaphorical connection between certain rivers and African Americans. After students reread the poem aloud, discuss their reactions to it. What was Hughes saying in this poem? How did the poem make them feel? What images came to their minds when they heard it read aloud? What did they learn from the poem? How are people like rivers? Who is the "I" in the poem?

⭐ **CREATIVE SPIRITS:** Langston Hughes once said that when he was happy, he didn't write anything. Ask students why they think that was so. Can they tie that statement to their own lives? How do they express themselves when they're unhappy? Do they feel better afterward? If students say that they don't do anything creative, talk about how expression might make them feel better.

Write About It

⭐ **DECLARING CLASS POETS:** As "class poet" in school, Hughes wrote his first poem. It included a verse for each of his teachers and all the students in his class—it was a *very* long poem. Make everyone in your class a class poet. Ask each student to contribute a verse of six to eight lines to a class poem. Let them arrange the verses in order and then post the entire poem on the wall.

⭐ **CREATING ODES:** Langston Hughes, like many poets, sometimes wrote poems of address. (This technique is also known as *apostrophe*, and poems written in this form are called *odes*.) Such poems speak directly to the subject, which is frequently an inanimate one. For an excellent example, read Hughes' poem entitled "Stars."

Explain to students that in a traditional ode, the subject is given honor or respect. Invite students to read and discuss the above poem and then try writing their own odes. If appropriate, review metaphor and simile before students begin to write. Invite students to share their odes by reading them aloud or illustrating and displaying their finished work. (Adapted from Judith Steinbergh's *Reading and Writing Poetry: A Guide for Teachers*, Scholastic, 1994.)

Be sure to give students opportunities to share their writing via read-alouds, bulletin boards, writing walls, learning centers, and so on.

Report About It

⭐ **FAVORITE POEMS:** Many of Langston Hughes' many poems were collected and published in book form. These include *First Book of Rhythms, Shakespeare in Harlem,* and *The Dream Keeper.* His poetry is still reprinted today in anthologies such as *Pass It On: African-American Poetry for Children* and *Make a Joyful Sound: Poems for Children by African-American Poets.* Let students select their favorite poems by Langston Hughes and by another poet. Ask them to compare the two poems and the two poets' lives. If possible, have students find out whether Langston Hughes and the other poets were contemporaries and, if so, whether they knew each other and what they thought of each other's work.

Report About It :

⭐ **FAVORITE POEMS:** Many of Langston Hughes' many poems were collected and published in book form. These include *First Book of Rhythms, Shakespeare in Harlem,* and *The Dream Keeper.* His poetry is still reprinted today in anthologies such as *Pass It On: African-American Poetry for Children* and *Make a Joyful Sound: Poems for Children by African-American Poets.* Let students select their favorite poems by Langston Hughes and by another poet. Ask them to compare the two poems and the two poets' lives. If possible, have students find out whether Langston Hughes and the other poets were contemporaries and, if so, whether they knew each other and what they thought of each other's work.

⭐ **MIRRORING THE WORLD:** In addition to writing poetry, Hughes produced short stories, plays, and articles. Ask students to find a sample of his work in another genre and prepare a report on it. Have them include the year in which it was written and where Hughes was living when he wrote the piece. What were some of the things that were happening in the world at the time? Does the work reflect that? Finally, have students explain why they think Hughes chose that particular form in which to express himself.

Rosa Parks and Martin Luther King, Jr.
The Montgomery Bus Boycott

by Shelli Milks

Characters (in order of appearance):

NARRATOR
AFRICAN AMERICAN MALE PASSENGERS 1-2
ROSA PARKS
JAMES BLAKE: White bus driver
AFRICAN AMERICAN FEMALE PASSENGERS 1-2
AFRICAN AMERICAN BUS PASSENGERS 1-4 (nonspeaking roles)
WHITE BUS PASSENGERS 1-8 (2 are speaking roles)
OFFICERS 1-3
JAIL MATRON
E.D. NIXON: President of the Mobile chapter of the NAACP
FRED GRAY: African American lawyer in Mobile, Alabama
RAYMOND "PARKS" PARKS: Rosa's husband
MEMBERS OF THE WOMEN'S POLITICAL COUNCIL 1-4
MARTIN LUTHER KING, JR.
REVEREND RALPH ABERNATHY

ACT 1

★★★★★ **SCENE:** December 1, 1955. Inside a city bus in Montgomery, Alabama.

(As the narrator speaks, people enter and exit the bus. Characters who are African American must pay first, then exit and re-enter through the side door. At the back of the bus there is a sign that reads, "THIS PART OF THE BUS FOR THE COLORED RACE.")

NARRATOR: Although slavery was declared illegal in the United States in 1863, many southern states put Jim Crow laws into effect. These laws kept the white and black populations separate. The two races used different water fountains and restrooms. They entered movie theaters by different doors. Inside, they sat in different sections. Under the Jim Crow laws, separate didn't mean equal. On public buses, African Americans were only allowed to sit or stand in the very back of the bus. Whenever there weren't enough seats in the white section of the bus, black people seated closest to the white section were expected to give up their seats.

(Rosa Parks steps onto the bus and pays her fare. She steps off and then re-enters through the back entrance. There is an African American man sitting next to the window, and Rosa sits next to him. There are two African American women sitting across the aisle from Rosa. A sign by Rosa's seat reads, "COLORED SECTION.")

ROSA (sighing): Oh, it feels so good to sit down. It's been a long day.

AFRICAN AMERICAN MALE PASSENGER 1: Hello, Mrs. Parks. It's a fine evening, isn't it?

ROSA: Yes, it is.

AFRICAN AMERICAN MALE PASSENGER 1: They keeping you busy at the department store?

ROSA (nodding): I believe everyone in Mobile needed a hem let down or new buttons sewn on their shirts this week.

AFRICAN AMERICAN FEMALE PASSENGER 1 (leaning across the aisle to speak to Rosa): Where's that NAACP workshop being held?

ROSA: We got rooms at Alabama State. I just found out tonight.

(The bus stops, several white people get on. They fill up the white section. Four white passengers are left standing.)

JAMES BLAKE (turning around and shouting): You got to give me those front seats!

(None of the people in the "Colored Section" move.)

JAMES BLAKE (standing up and shouting more loudly): Y'all better make it light on yourselves and give me those seats!

(The man beside Rosa gets out of his seat. Rosa moves her legs to let him pass. The two women across the aisle stand up reluctantly.)

JAMES BLAKE (to Rosa in a nasty tone): You better get a move on—right fast.

ROSA (looking him straight in the eye): I'm not moving.

JAMES BLAKE: You want me to call the police? They'll drag you down there to that police station. I'll give you two seconds . . . one—

ROSA (calmly, looking in front of her): I'm not moving.

AFRICAN AMERICAN MALE PASSENGER 2 (shouting from the back): You better move, Mrs. Parks!

AFRICAN AMERICAN FEMALE PASSENGER 1: She's going to get us all into trouble.

AFRICAN AMERICAN FEMALE PASSENGER 2: I'm so tired of these stupid rules! I wish I had the guts to stand up to them. (whispering) Don't move, Rosa. You stay right where you are.

(The bus driver sticks his head out of the window and whistles at a group of people on the sidewalk.)

JAMES BLAKE: Hey! You all call the police. I got a black woman in here who ain't giving up her seat.

(While waiting for the police, the passengers whisper to each other. Some leave the bus.)

WHITE PASSENGER 1 (to Rosa): Look, you know the rules. Why don't you just get up and go to the back? You'll be home before you know it.

WHITE PASSENGER 2 (to bus driver): I'll make her get up.

(There is the sound of a siren. Then three police officers board the bus.)

OFFICER 1: What's the problem?

JAMES BLAKE: That colored woman back there won't give up her seat.

OFFICER 1 (to Officer 2): Go get her.

OFFICER 2 (to Rosa): Why didn't you just stand up when you were supposed to?

ROSA: I'm tired. I pay the same money as anybody else. I deserve to sit down.

WHITE PASSENGER 2: You'll get to sit down all you want in jail!

OFFICER 2: You know the rules. What good does it do to break them?

(The officer escorts Rosa off the bus.)

ACT 2
★★★★★ SCENE: The Mobile police station.

ROSA: I'd like to make a phone call.

OFFICER 1: Forget about a phone call.

OFFICER 3 (behind desk, writing)**:** What's your name?

ROSA: Rosa Parks.

OFFICER 3: Address?

ROSA: 514 West Avenue.

OFFICER 3: Stand over there please. We have to take fingerprints and mug shots. (Rosa's prints are taken. She stands in front of a camera. Her mug shots are taken.) Matron, please take Mrs. Parks to her cell after she's made her phone call.

OFFICER 1: Come on—you're not going to let her make a call. She'll call what's-his-name at the NAACP. She works for him.

OFFICER 3: I think we can handle the NAACP. (He hands the telephone to Rosa.) One call. I have to ask you to make it short, ma'am.

ROSA (dialing number)**:** Parks, it's me. (pause) I'm in jail. (pause) No, I'm all right. They haven't hurt me. (pause) Just come and get me as quick as you can.

(After Rosa hangs up, the jail matron takes her to a cell. The telephone rings.)

OFFICER 1: Police station. (pause) Who? Parks? Rosa Parks? I don't know, let me check. (He hangs up the telephone.) That's what I call handling the NAACP.

ACT 3
★★★★★ SCENE: The Parks' living room.

NARRATOR: Word spread of Rosa's arrest. E.D. Nixon of the NAACP called the jail to find out what the charges were, but the officers wouldn't tell him. He also called Fred Gray, a local black lawyer. Gray agreed to help Rosa. Parks, Rosa's husband, called several friends to raise bail money for Rosa. They all went to the station. After Rosa was released that night, everyone gathered at the Parks' house.

E.D. NIXON: I know it's been a long day for you, Rosa, but we can't let what you did today go unnoticed. You're an honest woman. You have integrity. Everybody in Mobile knows that. Nobody could ever accuse you of any wrongdoing. You've given us a perfect test case against bus segregation. I know it's asking a lot. Will you do it, Rosa? Will you fight this thing for all of us?

ROSA: You bet I will.

NIXON: Parks, it's not going to be easy. Are you in this thing, too?

PARKS: I'm in. All the way.

FRED GRAY: We have to make this a big event. We need to do more than bring the case to court. I'm going to call Jo Ann Robinson and see if the Women's Political Council can help us organize a boycott of the buses.

PARKS: Then the white folks can have all the seats they want. Those buses will be more than half empty.

E.D. NIXON: I'd like to call in the Reverend Martin Luther King, Jr. from the Dexter Baptist Church. He's a powerful speaker. He'll get our message across.

(Nixon and Gray say good-bye and leave.)

PARKS: It looks like you've started something. They're right. It's not going to be easy.

ROSA: It's going to be easier than always having to give up your seat.

ACT 4
★★★★★★ **SCENE 1: December 2. A street corner in Montgomery.**

NARRATOR: The next day members of the Women's Political Council passed out handbills about the boycott on street corners and at bus stops.

(Women distribute handbills to passersby.)

WOMAN 1: Don't ride the bus on Monday!

WOMAN 2: A Negro woman has been arrested and put in jail because she refused to give up her seat!

WOMAN 3: If you work Monday, take a cab, share a ride, or walk. Call us and we'll help you get to work.

WOMAN 4: There's a meeting on Monday night at 7 o'clock at the Holt Street Baptist Church. Find out more about what we can do!

SCENE 2: December 5, 1955. The Holt Street Baptist Church.

NARRATOR: On Monday, December 5, 1955, the buses in Montgomery, Alabama, were empty! People who had cars gave rides to those who had no transportation. Many people walked. That night the Holt Street Baptist Church was packed with people who wanted to hear more about the boycott. Martin Luther King, Jr., leader of the newly formed Montgomery Improvement Association (M.I.A.), led the discussion.

MARTIN LUTHER KING, JR.: There comes a time when people get tired. We are here this evening to say we are tired of being kicked about.

(The crowd cheers in agreement.)

MARTIN LUTHER KING, JR.: We have nothing left to do but protest. Our protest will be nonviolent. Our method will be to persuade. We must remember what the Bible says: Love your enemies, bless them that curse you and pray for them that despitefully use you. We must not become bitter and end up hating all white people. As Booker T. Washington said: Let no man pull you so low as to make you hate him.

(The crowd cheers loudly.)

MARTIN LUTHER KING, JR.: I believe that today's boycott was successful. Now we need to decide whether or not to continue it. Please stand up if you want to keep it going.

(Everyone stands up. They then sit down.)

MARTIN LUTHER KING, JR.: Reverend Abernathy, please read the plans and rules we have drafted and let the people decide if this is what they want.

REV. ABERNATHY: Here are the conditions that must be met to end the boycott: Number one, all Negroes must receive polite treatment from the bus drivers; number two, all passengers must be seated on a first-come, first-served basis; and number three, Negro drivers should be hired for routes through Negro neighborhoods. All who agree with these conditions, please stand.

(Everyone stands up.)

REV. ABERNATHY: And now, let us show our gratitude to Mrs. Rosa Parks!

(The crowd cheers.)

NARRATOR: The Montgomery bus boycott lasted an entire year. During that time, Rosa Parks was in court several times. The Parks received bomb threats, and many Black churches were destroyed. On December 20, 1956, the United States Supreme Court ruled that Alabama's state and local laws requiring segregation on buses was against the Constitution. By refusing to give up her seat, Rosa Parks changed the course of history.

Rosa Parks and Martin Luther King, Jr.
Teaching Guide

Rosa McCauley was born in Tuskegee, Alabama, on February 4, 1913. Her father was a carpenter, and her mother was a teacher. Rosa met Raymond Parks, nicknamed "Parks," in 1931. He was a member of the National Association for the Advancement of Colored People and was very active in the group's efforts to obtain justice for African Americans wrongly accused of crimes. They married in August of 1932 and moved to Montgomery, Alabama. Rosa began doing volunteer work for the NAACP, as well. During the day, she worked as a seamstress, and Parks was a barber. After the bus boycott was over, Rosa and Parks moved to Detroit, Michigan. Parks died in 1977, but Rosa continues the work they started together through the Rosa and Raymond Parks Institute for Self-Development.

Martin Luther King, Jr., was born in Atlanta, Georgia, on January 15, 1929, to Alberta and Reverend Martin Luther King. His father was the minister of the Ebenezer Baptist Church. At college, Martin read about Mahatma Gandhi, and how he and his people had fought oppression by peaceful means. Nonviolence became his weapon in protesting segregation laws in the United States. Despite his peaceful approach, King was considered a threat by many white racists. Threats were made on his life; bombs were thrown at his house, endangering his family. On April 3, 1968, after giving one of his unifying and moving speeches in Memphis, Tennessee, Martin Luther King, Jr. was assassinated. His work is remembered every year on his birthday, January 15, Martin Luther King, Jr. Day.

Book Links

Rosa Parks by Eloise Greenfield, illustrated by Eric Marlow (Thomas Y. Crowell, 1973)

Rosa Parks: My Story by Rosa Parks, with Jim Haskins (Dial Books, 1992)

Martin Luther King: The Peaceful Warrior by Ed Clayton (Silver Burdett, 1991)

Meet Martin Luther King, Jr. by James T. De Kay (Random House, 1989)

Young Martin's Promise by Walter D. Myers (Raintree Steck-Vaughn, 1992)

EXTENSION ACTIVITIES

Talk About It

⭐ **DISCUSS BOYCOTTS:** The word *boycott* comes from the name of Irish landowner Charles C. Boycott, who was ostracized for not lowering rents on his property in 1897. Discuss the bus boycott in Montgomery and its results. Do students think a boycott is an effective form of protest? Ask them to consider what would happen if people stopped shopping at a local store. What would happen to the people who own the store? How would the boycott affect the workers and their families? In what ways would the rest of the community be touched? What kinds of sacrifices would people on both sides of the boycott have to make?

⭐ **HELPING HANDS:** When she refused to give up her seat, Rosa Parks started a chain reaction of change. Have students recap the action in the play. Discuss the fact that the actions of one person caused other people to react. Do students feel that one person can make a difference? Then talk about the issues that most concern your class. Encourage small groups of students to concentrate on different issues, such as the environment, racism, homelessness, or refugees from war-torn countries. Each group should talk about why they are concerned about the situation and then create a detailed plan of what they can do to change it. Have all groups share their plans of action.

Write About It

⭐ **CREATE LEAFLETS:** The Women's Political Caucus handed out leaflets to spread news about the Montgomery bus boycott. Before students begin the following activity, discuss leaflets with them. Do they recall any leaflets they have seen? If so, why do those in particular stick in their minds? Mention that since the amount of space on a leaflet is limited, the message has to be short; only the most pertinent information is included, and illustrations and graphics are used to highlight certain things. Have students write and design their own leaflets telling about Rosa Parks, the boycott, the reason for it, and the meeting at the church.

⭐ **RIDE THE BUS:** The Montgomery bus was crowded on December 1, 1955, but ask students to take a ride on that bus. Let them imagine that they're very tired and that they just want to get home and eat dinner. What would they say to Rosa Parks to make her stop her protest? Then encourage students to pretend that they are a sympathetic passenger on the bus who joins Rosa's protest. What would they say to encourage other people to join them? Students writings may take the form of monologues or dialogues.

Be sure to give students opportunities to share their writing via read-alouds, bulletin boards, writing walls, learning centers, and so on.

Report About It

⭐ **SQUELCH SEGREGATION:** The Jim Crow laws that existed consisted of laws actually on the books, as well as "unwritten" laws traditionally sanctioned by a community. Make a copy of the United States Constitution available to students. Discuss the sections that deal with human rights. Ask students why they think the segregation laws were finally declared unconstitutional. Then have them research important civil rights cases. Remind students to include the courts' dissenting opinions in their reports.

⭐ **CIVIL RIGHTS REPORTERS:** The NAACP in Alabama was also involved in the formation of the Brotherhood of Sleeping Car Porters and the Alabama Voter's League. The civil rights movement of the 1960s encompassed many history-changing events, including the march to Washington, D.C. and a sit-in at a lunch counter in Greensboro, North Carolina. Have groups of two to three students choose events in the struggle for civil rights and report on them as news teams would by reporting different areas of information and then taking turns reporting what they found.

Jackie Robinson
At Home in the Major Leagues

≋

by Justin Martin

Characters (in order of appearance):

NARRATOR
BRANCH RICKEY: President of the Brooklyn Dodgers
JACKIE ROBINSON
ENOS SLAUGHTER: Cardinals left fielder
TERRY MOORE: Cardinals center fielder
PEEWEE REESE: Captain of the Brooklyn Dodgers
GEORGE MUNGER: Cardinals pitcher (nonspeaking role)
FANS 1-6
ANNOUNCER
NEWSPAPER REPORTERS 1-3
PHOTOGRAPHERS 1-3 (nonspeaking roles)

ACT 1

★★★★★ SCENE: 1947. Branch Rickey's office in Brooklyn, New York.

NARRATOR: Prior to 1947, baseball was divided by race. Black players were not allowed to play on major-league teams such as the New York Yankees or the Chicago Cubs. Instead, they played in the Negro League, which was composed of teams like the Kansas City Monarchs and the Birmingham Black Barons. A meeting between Branch Rickey, the Brooklyn Dodgers president, and a talented young black ballplayer named Jackie Robinson was to change all of that.

RICKEY: Any idea why I called you here, Jackie?

JACKIE: I thought probably you were going to offer me a chance to play in the Negro League. Maybe something with the Brooklyn Brown Dodgers.

RICKEY: No. I want you to play in the Majors. For the Brooklyn Dodgers. It's time to put an end to this color barrier thing. Black players should play in the Majors. You're just the ballplayer to—

JACKIE: Hold on a minute. The majors? Are you kidding?

RICKEY: Look—I'm not saying it's going to be easy. Fans may boo when you walk out onto the field. Other players may call you names. Pitchers may throw the ball at your head. But whatever happens, you *cannot* lose your temper. Got that?

JACKIE: Mr. Rickey, are you looking for a player who doesn't have the guts to fight back?

RICKEY: Not all, Jackie. I'm looking for a player with guts enough *not* to fight back!

JACKIE (thinking for a moment and then nodding his head): You've got yourself a deal.

ACT 2

★★★★★ SCENE: Dodgers Stadium, in Brooklyn, New York. The Brooklyn Dodgers vs. the Saint Louis Cardinals.

NARRATOR: During the warm-up period before a baseball game, players usually visit with their friends on the other team. The Dodgers-Cardinals game was no exception. The players mingled, talking and laughing. Jackie Robinson and his friend PeeWee Reese walked over to where two Cardinal outfielders, Enos Slaughter and Terry Moore, were standing. PeeWee shook Slaughter's hand and then Moore's. Jackie Robinson held out his hand . . .

(Robinson reaches out to shake Enos Slaughter's hand.)

SLAUGHTER (pulling away his hand): No way. I ain't shaking no black man's hand.

MOORE: Goes double for me. I don't want his skin color rubbing off on me.

SLAUGHTER: Good one, Terry!

(They laugh and high-five each other.)

NARRATOR: Jackie started to say something, but then he remembered Branch Rickey's advice. As he walked away, PeeWee put his arm around Jackie to show the other players and the fans that they were friends.

PEEWEE: Don't let it get to you, Jackie. Slaughter and Moore are just narrow-minded fools. They're not even worth worrying about.

JACKIE: That may be true, but what they said still hurts me.

PEEWEE: You've just got to ignore those two bozos. Knock the ball out of the park—that'll show 'em.

NARRATOR: Brooklyn fans were famous for being some of the meanest fans around. When Jackie came up to bat, many of the hometown fans were as unfriendly as Slaughter and Moore had been.

(Jackie walks to home plate to bat against Cardinals pitcher George Munger. Most of the fans greet him with boos.)

FANS 2-6: Boooo! Robinson, you're nothing but a bum! Boooooo! Go back to where you came from, ya bum!

FAN 1: Yaaay! Go Jackie! Out of the park, slugger! Come on, come on!

ANNOUNCER: George Munger goes into his windup. And here's the pitch. Robinson hits the ball hard! It's headed toward deep center field! Slaughter and Moore are going back, they're going waaay back! The ball's over their heads! It's going to roll all the way to the wall . . . there it goes! Robinson's running fast! There he goes—around first base and headed for second! Slaughter's just now getting to the ball. And Robinson's *still* going—he's around second, headed for third! And he makes it! Jackie Robinson has a triple!"

FANS 1-3: Yaaay! Way to go Robinson! Bring it home, Jackie! Come on home!

FANS 4-6: Boooo! Robinson's nothing but a bum! Boooooo! Throw him out!

NARRATOR: In major league baseball, when a player is standing on third base, it's possible for him to run home while the pitcher is throwing a pitch. This is called stealing home. It's one of the most difficult feats in baseball. Robinson's great speed made him a master at stealing home. He stole home 19 times in his career.

(PeeWee Reese steps up to the plate to face George Munger.)

ANNOUNCER: Robinson's at third; PeeWee Reese is at the plate. Munger looks over and checks on Robinson. Now he goes into his windup, kicks high—wait a minute!

172

There goes Robinson! He's trying to steal home! Here comes Munger's pitch! Here comes Robinson! He slides—he's sliding—he's sliding—he's safe! Holy cow, Robinson's stolen home! The Dodgers score!

FANS 1-5: Yaaay Jackie! Way to go!

FAN 6: Booooo! Robinson, you're still a bum! Booooo!

(The other five fans stop cheering and stare at Fan 6 until he or she finally gets the message. Then Fan 6 starts cheering, too.)

FANS 1-6: Yaaay Jackie! Robinson's our man!

PEEWEE (shaking Jackie's hand): Way to go, Jackie!

NARRATOR: Jackie and PeeWee walked off the field toward the dugout. Members of the press came running out to meet them. In their excitement, the reporters kept interrupting each other. Meanwhile, photographers jumped around, snapping pictures of Jackie and PeeWee.

REPORTER 1: Jackie, what do you—

REPORTER 2: Hey, Jackie, tell us about—

REPORTER 3 (shouting above the other two reporters): Jackie, how does it feel to be the first black player in major league baseball?

JACKIE: It's a great honor—and a great responsibility. I hope that my accomplishments will help make it possible for other black people to pursue their dreams.

ACT 3
★★★★★ **SCENE: Yankee Stadium in the Bronx, New York; opening game of the 1947 World Series.**

NARRATOR: The 1947 season was a challenge to Robinson. Although it was one of the toughest seasons that anyone has ever had to face, Jackie excelled. He was named Rookie of the Year, and he helped the Dodgers reach the World Series. The Dodgers were up against their arch rivals, the New York Yankees. Standing in Yankee Stadium in the opening game of the World Series, Jackie had an experience that he would later remember as the most important of his life.

(As "The Star Spangled Banner" is sung, Jackie and PeeWee stand side by side, with their hands on their hearts. PeeWee drops his hand immediately when the song is over and looks over at Jackie. Robinson's hand is still over his heart; he slowly lets it fall to his side.)

PEEWEE: Jackie—you all right, man?

JACKIE: Yeah.

PEEWEE: You sure?

JACKIE: It's just . . . while "The Star Spangled Banner" was playing, I had this whole new feeling. It's like I heard the song for the first time. I finally felt like it was being played for me, too.

PEEWEE: Well, sure, that's how it should be.

JACKIE: Yeah, that's how it *should* be. And today it was. (slapping PeeWee on the back) Now let's go get those Yankees!

NARRATOR: Thanks to Jackie Robinson, other black ballplayers, including such players as Hank Aaron and Willie Mays, broke into the major leagues. Jackie Robinson will always be remembered for taking one of the first and most important steps toward making all Americans feel that they are part of "the land of the free."

Jackie Robinson
Teaching Guide

Jack Roosevelt "Jackie" Robinson was born on January 31, 1919, in a small town in Georgia. He moved to Pasadena, California, when he was very young. Later he attended the University of California at Los Angeles where he was a stand-out in baseball, football, basketball, and track. While at UCLA, Robinson met Rachel Isum who later became his wife. After college, he played for the Kansas City Monarchs in the Negro Leagues. In 1947, Jackie had a private meeting with Branch Rickey, president of the Brooklyn Dodgers. Rickey explained that he thought Jackie was the right player to break the color barrier which kept African Americans out of major league baseball. On April 15, 1947, Jackie played his first game for the Dodgers against the Boston Braves. He went on to win the Rookie of the Year Award that season. Other highlights of Robinson's ten-year career include playing on six all-star teams and winning a Most Valuable Player Award in 1949. After retiring, he received the highest honor in baseball, election to the Hall of Fame. Jackie Robinson died in 1972 at the age of 53.

Book Links

Thank You, Jackie Robinson by Barbara Cohen (Lothrop, 1988)

Teammates by Peter Golenbock (Harcourt Brace Jovanovich, 1990)

Jackie Robinson by Richard Scott (Chelsea House, 1987)

EXTENSION ACTIVITIES

Talk About It

⭐ **THE TALENT POOL:** Jackie Robinson was and still is a hero to many people. Ask students to name their favorite sports heroes. Write their responses on the chalkboard. Your list might go something like this: Michael Jordan, Florence Griffith Joyner, Larry Bird, Bo Jackson, Joe Montana, Charles Barkley, Dave Winfield, Nancy Kerrigan, and so on. When the list is complete, silently erase the names of all the African American athletes, one by one. After you've finished, the list will be substantially shorter. Let students tell you what the erased heroes have in common. Discuss what the world of sports would be like today if Jackie Robinson hadn't broken the color barrier.

☆ **THINK-IT-THROUGH CARDS:** What might have happened if Jackie Robinson had lost his temper and fought back (in the traditional sense) when the other players and fans demonstrated their prejudice? Did Robinson fight back in his own way? Divide students into groups of four or five, and have them discuss this question: What does it mean to "fight back?" After groups have had ample time to explore this question, give each a 3-by-5-inch index card with a different scenario printed on it, such as: "A bully threatens to beat you up if you don't hand over your milk money. Should you fight back?" Let groups talk about the question and decide what they would do. Finally, bring all of the groups together to share their decisions. Take notes on their responses and then read them aloud. This verbal summary will give students the opportunity to reflect on their choices. Do any of the groups revise their decisions?

Write About It

☆ **RIGHTING WRONGS:** Jackie Robinson's good friend, PeeWee Reese, called Enos Slaughter and Terry Moore "narrow-minded" because they did not want to play baseball with an African American man. Ask students to write about what they think it means to be narrow-minded. Have they ever had a bad experience because of a person who was narrow-minded? How did they handle the situation? If students were dissatisfied by their responses, suggest that they write a dialogue between themselves and that person.

☆ **ANTHEM ESSAYS:** After becoming an accepted major league baseball player, Jackie Robinson told PeeWee Reese: "I finally felt like it [the National Anthem] was being played for me, too." Play "The Star Spangled Banner" for your class. Ask students to listen and to imagine they are Jackie Robinson. Then have them write an essay or journal entry from Jackie's point of view: What do the words mean? How does the song make them feel? Also encourage students to set down how the song personally affects them. Do they feel that it has meaning in their lives?

Be sure to give students opportunities to share their writing via read-alouds, bulletin boards, writing walls, learning centers, and so on.

Report About It

☆ **PLAYER TRADING CARDS:** Encourage students to research all the people involved in the play: Branch Rickey, PeeWee Reese, Enos Slaughter, Terry Moore, George Munger, and, of course, Jackie Robinson. Students can then create trading cards—complete with pictures and biographies—for each of these history makers. When they are finished, students may use the cards to retell the story of Jackie Robinson.

☆ **CIVIL RIGHTS COUNT DOWN:** Invite students to research the key events that have contributed to the breakdown of the color barrier in the United States and present that information in the form of a time line. Students may choose to represent only sports-related events or a more comprehensive history of the civil rights movement.

Cesar Chavez

!Viva La Causa!

by Jaime Lucero

Characters (in order of appearance):

NARRATOR
CESAR CHAVEZ
LIBRADO CHAVEZ: Cesar's father
JUANA CHAVEZ: Cesar's mother
FRED ROSS
MIGRANT WORKERS 1-5
REPORTER
FARMER WILSON

ACT 1
★★★★★ SCENE: June 1937. The Chavez farm near Yuma, Arizona.

NARRATOR: In 1937, during the Great Depression, times were hard for most Americans. Prices for common goods were high, while wages hit an all-time low. Farmers, especially, suffered. Markets were oversupplied with fruits and vegetables. As a result, farm prices dropped to their lowest in 50 years. Many farm owners were unable to pay their bills, and they lost their land. The Depression hit the Chavez family. One afternoon ten-year-old Cesar walked into his house and found his father sitting at the kitchen table instead of working in the fields. His mother had opened all the drawers and cabinets in the kitchen. She was packing the dishes and silverware.

CESAR: What's happening? Mama, what are you doing? Why are you packing?

LIBRADO: We can't pay the bills. The bank's taken over the farm.

CESAR: No! I'm not leaving! I don't want to go!

JUANA: Cesar, *hijito*, go pack your bag. We have no choice. Nobody in Yuma has any money. They can't buy what we've grown.

CESAR: Someone'll help us—

LIBRADO: Who? Our friends and families can't help. They're as bad off as we are. We already owe the bank money—money I can't pay.

CESAR: But where will we go? Where will we live?

LIBRADO: I'll ask other farmers for work. We'll follow the crops.

CESAR: Follow the crops? What does that mean? They don't go anywhere.

LIBRADO: It means we travel across the country, we follow the trail of the different crops as they ripen. We'll begin by picking cotton in Texas. When the cotton's all picked, we'll come back to Arizona and then California to pick grapes.

JUANA: Go on and pack, Cesar. We have to leave soon.

NARRATOR: Cesar had to leave his friends and the only home he'd ever known behind. Many families in the southwest were forced to make the same choice that Cesar's family had to make. Overnight, they changed from farm *owners* to farm *workers*. Because they "migrated" with the crops, these workers came to be known as migrant workers.

ACT 2
★★★★★ SCENE: 1938. A farm in southeastern California.

NARRATOR: Migrant families were often mistreated, overworked, and unfairly paid. It was common to find several families in one small, filthy shack. Farm owners purposely kept the living conditions unpleasant so that migrant families wouldn't get comfortable and feel too rooted. There were no set wages for migrant workers so farm owners paid whatever they pleased. Sometimes workers were paid with food, and sometimes with money. Since migrant workers were paid by the amount of fruits and vegetables they picked, it was not unusual to see an entire family— including children—working in the fields. Cesar learned to pick grapes and other fruits at a very young age.

LIBRADO: You and your brothers and sisters have worked hard, Cesar. Once I collect our wages for the week, I'll take all of you to the movies.

CESAR: Can we have popcorn, too?

LIBRADO: Of course!

NARRATOR: When he and his father arrived at the farmer's house, Cesar noticed that the man's truck was gone. Cesar's father knocked on the door. There was no answer. He knocked harder. The front door swung open. Cesar looked inside the house.

CESAR: Papa, look! There's no one living here.

LIBRADO (angrily): We've been swindled!

CESAR: Swindled? I don't understand.

LIBRADO: Cheated! The man's moved away so he wouldn't have to pay us. He knows we can't wait around for him to come back. We have to move on to the next crop.

CESAR: That's not fair! What are we going to do?

LIBRADO: Nothing. There's no law against this. We're migrant workers. We've got no protection against this.

CESAR: What do we do now?

LIBRADO: We move on, and we hope that the next farmer treats us fairly.

ACT 3
★★★★★ SCENE 1: 1952. Sal Si Puedes, California. Cesar Chavez's home.

NARRATOR: The years passed. Young Cesar grew up. He married and had a family of his own. Although times were still hard for Cesar, he managed to save enough money to buy a small home in the poor community of Sal Si Puedes, which translates to "Get out, if you can." The migrant workers' situation hadn't changed much. Then one day a man named Fred Ross knocked on Cesar Chavez's front door.

FRED: Are you Cesar Chavez?

CESAR: Yes. How can I help you?

FRED: My name is Fred Ross. I'm an organizer for the Community Services Organization. We're a private agency that helps farm workers. Migrant workers have been treated unfairly for years—

CESAR: You don't have to convince *me* of that.

FRED: I need your help. Can you arrange a meeting and invite every farm worker in the area? It's time to put an end to bad working conditions.

NARRATOR: Cesar thought over what Fred Ross said. He thought of his father losing the farm, and of himself growing up in one filthy shack after another. He thought of all the schools he had had to leave because the crops were in, and they'd had to move.

CESAR: Okay. I'll do it.

FRED (shaking Cesar's hand)**:** Oh, one more thing. You'll have to do the talking.

CESAR: What?! Me? No way!

FRED: You know what it's like to be a migrant worker. Who's going to listen to me?

CESAR: I just did.

FRED: You know what I mean.

CESAR: What am I supposed to say?

FRED: Don't worry. You'll find the words.

SCENE 2 : Cesar's home later that week.

CESAR: *Amigos y amigas, buenas tardes.* My name is Cesar Chavez. Like most of you, I'm a migrant worker. For too many years we have witnessed too many *injusticias* brought against us and our families. It's time for things to change!

NARRATOR: Cesar immediately created a stir among the people at his home. The migrant workers present knew that unlike other labor workers, they had no union to support them. It would be very hard for them to organize and to force the farmers to pay attention to them.

180

MIGRANT WORKER 1: I don't think the farmers would be too happy if they knew we were meeting here today.

MIGRANT WORKER 2: He's right. I think we should leave.

MIGRANT WORKER 3: I have a family to support and feed. I can't afford to cause any trouble.

CESAR: It's not trouble that we're asking for—it's justice!

NARRATOR: Several migrant workers stood up and headed for the door. Cesar didn't know how to stop them. He nervously looked over to Fred Ross for help, but then he had an idea.

CESAR: Wait! You—there by the door. How old are you?

MIGRANT WORKER 4: Me? Forty-five. Why?

CESAR: What would you say if I told you that you only have four years left to live?

MIGRANT WORKER 4: *Que?* What? You're crazy!

FRED: No, Cesar's right. According to statistics, the average migrant worker lives to the age of 49. The average American lives to be almost 70.

(The migrant workers look at each other and then return to their seats.)

CESAR: Do you know why our time is so short? The answer is right before you, *amigos.* Just think of your living and working conditions.

MIGRANT WORKER 5: My living conditions *are* bad—they're crowded and cramped. There's two families living in my shack!

MIGRANT WORKER 1: That's nothing! There's three families living with us!

MIGRANT WORKER 2: My roof is so bad that the wind comes in every night off the desert. You all know how cold it is . . . that's why my little Jose died of pneumonia last year.

CESAR: We have to protect our families. We have to protect ourselves.

MIGRANT WORKER 3: Working conditions are just as bad. I cough all the time. It's those pesticides they use to keep the bugs off the crops.

MIGRANT WORKER 4: I've fainted twice—twice!—from working too long under the hot sun.

MIGRANT WORKER 5: Me, too. I'm always coughing, and I've fainted in the fields, but I can't afford a doctor.

CESAR: Do you see what's happening here? What have we done to be treated this way? Nothing!

MIGRANT WORKERS 1-5: Yes, that's right! Nothing! We're all being treated unfairly! Worse than the bugs they spray!

CESAR: It's time for things to change!

MIGRANT WORKERS 1-5: But how? What can we do? The farmers are too powerful.

CESAR: We organize and form a union! Then the farmers will see what power is!

MIGRANT WORKERS 1-5: Yes! Yes! *¡Viva La Causa!* Long live the cause!

NARRATOR: Cesar Chavez and his family stopped working in the fields. He began devoting all his time to *La Causa* (the Cause). Many farm workers and generous people in the community banded together to help support the Chavezes.

ACT 4
★★★★★ **SCENE 1: 1965. Outside a local farm in southern California.**

NARRATOR: With the help of many people, Cesar Chavez was successful in organizing the union for farm workers, which came to be known as the National Farm Workers Association (NFWA). He and the workers petitioned, participated in strikes, marched, organized, and held peaceful rallies. Chavez was popular among migrant workers, but the farmers hated him. It wasn't until the famous Grape Boycott which began in 1966 that Cesar Chavez gained international attention.

MIGRANT WORKERS 1-5 (carrying picket signs and marching in a small circle): Boycott grapes! Don't eat grapes! *¡Viva La Causa!*

REPORTER: Here we are in sunny California with Cesar Chavez and a local farmer. Both have agreed to an interview. Mr. Chavez, can you tell us what's happening here?

CESAR: We're asking people not to buy or eat grapes.

REPORTER: But why?

CESAR: If people stop eating grapes, the farmers won't be able to sell their crops to anyone.

REPORTER: But that would make farmers lose money. Why do you want to hurt the farmers of America?

CESAR: Because after years and years of loyal service, the migrant worker is still being mistreated.

FARMER WILSON: Now hold on a minute, Chavez! I've never mistreated any one of you.

CESAR: Then why not listen to what we have to say?

182

REPORTER: And what is that, Cesar?

CESAR: We demand better working and living conditions—and a guaranteed minimum wage for every worker.

FARMER WILSON: It can't be done. We'll go out of business. If there aren't any more farmers, who'll you work for then?

SCENE 2: June 14, 1969. Outside Wilson's farm in southern California.

NARRATOR: It took years, but eventually the Grape Boycott was a success. People from California to New York took part in the protest. All across the country people stopped buying grapes. As demand for grapes dropped, so did the prices. This proved devastating to the grape farmers of California.

MIGRANT WORKERS 1-5 (carrying picket signs while marching in a small circle): Boycott grapes! Don't eat grapes! Send a message to the farmers! *Viva La Causa!* Better conditions for the farm workers!

REPORTER: Mr. Wilson, you've called this meeting. Why?

FARMER WILSON (to Cesar): My business is suffering. I haven't been able to sell my grapes for weeks. Nobody's eating grapes. They're just sitting there, rotting on the vine.

MIGRANT WORKERS 1-5: Yaay! ¡*Viva La Causa!*

FARMER WILSON: I'm ready to listen to what you have to say.

NARRATOR: The Grape Boycott officially came to an end on June 14, 1969. The following year the nation's first table-grape labor contract was signed. This contract provided a wage increase and health insurance for farm workers. It also included regulations against the use of certain pesticides, such as DDT. Cesar Chavez continued to fight for the rights of all farm workers until the day of his death on April 22, 1993.

Cesar Chavez
Teaching Guide

Cesario ("Cesar") Estrada Chavez was born on March 31, 1927, on a small farm near Yuma, Arizona. He was the eldest of five children. Cesar was ten years old when his family lost its farm and had to join the ranks of the migrant workers who "followed the crops." After attending more than 30 schools, Cesar graduated from eighth grade, his last year of formal schooling. He joined the U.S. Navy in 1944 and married Helen Fabela in 1948. After meeting Fred Ross, Cesar joined the Community Service Organization (CSO). He started out as an organizer and eventually became executive director. In 1962, he established the National Farm Workers Association (NFWA) which later became the United Farm Workers (UFW), and organized California grape pickers in what became a five-year strike. In 1966, Chavez led a march from Delano to Sacramento, California. This focus of attention on the plight of grape pickers began a nationwide consumer boycott of grapes from California to New York. The boycott proved successful as it forced grape growers to sign contracts that guaranteed migrant workers better wages and a better way of life. The grape boycott officially ended on June 14, 1969. Chavez died on April 22, 1993 at San Luis, Arizona.

Book Links

Mighty Hard Road by James Terzian and Kathryn Cramer (Doubleday, 1970)

Cesar Chavez: Farm Worker Activist by Burnham Holmes (Steck-Vaughn, 1994)

Hispanics of Achievement: Cesar Chavez by Consuelo Rodriguez (Chelsea House, 1991)

EXTENSION ACTIVITIES

Talk About It

☆ **SACRIFICE FOR A CAUSE:** The success of the Grape Boycott depended upon the American people. If no one stopped buying and eating grapes, then the United Farm Workers wouldn't have succeeded. How many of your students count grapes as one of their favorite foods? If the boycott were in force today, would they be willing to stop eating grapes? Why or why not? Extend the discussion by asking students to name their favorite foods. For which causes would they be willing to give up those foods? Encourage students to think of slogans for their boycotts.

Write About It

⭐ **CREATE A CORRIDA:** A *corrida* is a ballad that celebrates the exploits of a hero. In Mexico, before telephones, radios, and televisions linked communities, these songs were passed from person to person and news spread in this way. Have students write a *corrida* that tells the story of Cesar Chavez's life.

⭐ **ACTION LETTERS:** Although Cesar Chavez has passed away, the work of the UFW continues. The migrant workers have won many concessions, but their lives are still hard. Invite students to write a letter to the union asking about its current concerns. The address is: United Farm Workers of America/ UFW, AFL-CIO, P.O. Box 62, Keene, CA 93531.

Be sure to give students opportunities to share their writing via read-alouds, bulletin boards, writing walls, learning centers, and so on.

Report About It

⭐ **CLASS MURALS:** The Mexican artist Diego Rivera, among others, is famous for his murals which depict the history of Mexico. The mural-making tradition is carried on in Latino communities in the United States. Have students find out more about migrant workers, Cesar Chavez, and the United Farm Workers. They may wish to focus on current conditions for workers; Chavez himself, including his hunger strikes; or other members of the UFW, such as Dolores Huerta. Let them use their research to create a mural in your classroom depicting the struggles of the farm workers.

⭐ **KENNEDY CONNECTION:** Cesar Chavez and Robert Kennedy had a special relationship. After Kennedy's death, his widow Ethel continued to support Chavez. Ask students to document the friendship between these two men and to contrast their childhoods.

⭐ **CROP MAPS:** Because Cesar and his family "followed the crops," he attended more than 30 schools. What kinds of crops in the United States are harvested by migrant workers? In which areas are these crops located? After students find the answers to these questions, have them present their findings on maps of the United States. Ask them to show the routes families might take as they follow the crops.

Neil Armstrong
To the Moon!

by Timothy Nolan

Characters (in order of appearance):

NARRATOR 1-2
NASA COMMANDER
NEIL ARMSTRONG
JANET ARMSTRONG: Neil's wife
EDWIN "BUZZ" ALDRIN: Astronaut on the Apollo 11 mission
MICHAEL COLLINS: Astronaut on the Apollo 11 mission
TECHNICIAN
VOICE OF MISSION CONTROL

ACT 1

★★★★★★ **SCENE: January 1969. An office at Mission Control. The NASA commander sits at his desk. Neil Armstrong is standing in front of the desk.**

NARRATOR 1: In 1961, President John F. Kennedy told the American people that he wanted the United States to land a man on the moon by 1970. To accomplish this, the National Aeronautics and Space Administration (NASA) created Project Mercury, the first space-flight program. Project Mercury put the first Americans in space. It was so successful that NASA started Project Gemini to test many of the space ships and procedures that would be used in a launch to the moon. One of the astronauts who tested these ships was Neil Armstrong.

NARRATOR 2: On March 16, 1966, he and crewman David Scott successfully docked *Gemini 8* with an orbiting space craft. Suddenly, after disconnecting, *Gemini 8* spun out of control! The radio, the astronauts's only connection to earth, also went dead. Neil Armstrong took the controls and successfully piloted *Gemini 8* back to Earth. He was awarded a medal for his skillful flying.

NARRATOR 1: More challenges lay ahead for Neil Armstrong.

NASA COMMANDER: We've chosen Michael Collins as the pilot for *Apollo 11* and Buzz Aldrin as the specialist, but we still don't have a commander for the crew.

NEIL: Well, sir, I know a lot of good pilots who could do the job.

NASA COMMANDER: I didn't call you in here to hear your recommendations, Neil.

NEIL: Sorry, sir.

NASA COMMANDER: I want you to command the flight.

NEIL: Me?!

NASA COMMANDER: We saw how you handled *Gemini 8.* You saved your life and Scott's. You brought the ship back. Your work has allowed Project Apollo to succeed—so far. Now it's time to do what we set out to do—put a man on the moon. We'd like you to be that man, Neil.

NEIL: Sir, I'm a civilian. I'm not in the military—

NASA COMMANDER: I need the best pilot in the world for this trip. That's you. We need you, Neil. Your country needs you.

NEIL (thinking a moment and then answering): I would be honored, sir.

ACT 2

★★★★★ **SCENE 1: July 15, 1969. The astronauts' quarters. Neil and his two Apollo 11 crewmen, Mike Collins and Buzz Aldrin, are inside. Neil is on the phone with his wife, Janet.**

NARRATOR 1: Ten days before the launch of *Apollo 11* the crew is isolated. They can't have any visitors. Food is brought into their quarters by people wearing special suits. Mission briefings are done through glass.

NARRATOR 2: NASA isn't worried about the crew backing out. They don't want Armstrong, Collins, and Aldrin going to the moon with sore throats.

NARRATOR 1: The men's only contact with their families is by telephone.

NEIL: How are the boys?

JANET: They're fine. They miss you, though. I do, too.

NEIL: I miss you all, too. I wish sometimes they'd picked someone else to command the mission.

JANET: They couldn't. They needed the best pilot. That's you.

NEIL: I don't know about "best."

JANET: I can see the moon from the living room window. It's so strange to think that you'll be there soon.

(The NASA Commander enters. He is wearing a special protective suit.)

NEIL: The commander just came in, honey, I have to go.

JANET: I'll be looking for you on the moon. Just make sure you come back home safe and sound.

NEIL: I will. I promise.

(Neil hangs up the phone. He joins Mike, Buzz, and the commander.)

COMMANDER: How are you fellows doing?

BUZZ: Great!

MIKE: Terrific!

NEIL: Fine. Ready to fly.

COMMANDER: Good. I just came in to tell you that a landing site on the moon has been selected. It's a large crater called the Sea of Tranquility.

BUZZ: Lucky for us there's no water in it!

COMMANDER: It's a huge crater, as wide as a football field and several miles long. It

looks smooth enough for a lunar landing. Mike, you'll stay in the command module and orbit the moon. Neil and Buzz, you'll fly the *Eagle*, and land it down in the Sea of Tranquility. The computer will guide you to the landing point.

NEIL: I thought *we* were going to fly it down.

COMMANDER: Well, of course you and Buzz will monitor the computer, but it'll be doing the actual flying. We need you to land at that exact spot. It looks like there aren't any large rocks there.

BUZZ: Rocks are a problem?

COMMANDER: They could break one of the *Eagle's* legs or make the module fall over on its side when you land. Fellows, if something happens to the *Eagle*, there's no way we can rescue you. You know that. You'll be stranded on the moon forever.

NEIL: Don't worry—we'll find a smooth spot.

COMMANDER: Just trust the computer and you'll be fine. Now get some sleep—you lift off in the morning.

SCENE 2: July 16, 1969. The launch pad at Cape Kennedy. Neil, Buzz, and Mike are strapped into the command module Columbia by a technician.

TECHNICIAN: You guys okay?

(The three astronauts give the "thumbs up" sign.)

NEIL: Ready to go!

TECHNICIAN: Okay, guys. Good luck!

(The technician closes and seals the door. He steps backward through another door and closes it.)

VOICE OF MISSION CONTROL: T minus eight seconds . . . seven . . . six . . . five . . . four . . . three . . . two . . . one . . . lift off!

ACT 3

★★★★★ **SCENE 1: July 20, 1969. Aboard Apollo 11. Mike is piloting the command module. Neil and Buzz have moved to the Eagle, the lunar module.**

NARRATOR 1: With Mike Collins at the controls of the command module the *Columbia*, Neil Armstrong and Buzz Aldrin climb into the *Eagle*. Collins will orbit the moon while Neil and Buzz are on the moon. They will then fly the *Eagle* back to the *Columbia* and begin the trip home.

189

NARRATOR 2: Once the *Eagle* detaches from the *Columbia*, the lunar module will be on its own. If something goes wrong, Neil and Buzz will be lost in space.

NEIL: *Eagle* to *Columbia*. We're on our way.

MIKE: See you both in a couple of days. Have fun on the moon. Bring me back some green cheese.

BUZZ: Don't go anywhere without us.

NEIL: Apollo 11 to Mission Control.

MISSION CONTROL: Go ahead, Apollo 11.

NEIL: Mission Control, the *Eagle* has wings. We are en route to the moon.

MISSION CONTROL: Roger, *Eagle*. We are engaging the on-board computer.

NEIL: Roger, Mission Control.

BUZZ: Looks like we get to sit back and enjoy the ride.

NEIL: Let's hope so.

NARRATOR 1: Neil and Buzz monitor their instruments and look out the window of the *Eagle*. From a distance, the Sea of Tranquility looks like a large, open patch on the lunar landscape. But as the crater gets closer, the astronauts see one large rock. Then another. And another.

BUZZ: Uh-oh. Neil, take a look at this.

NEIL: What is it?

BUZZ: The Sea of Tranquility—it's full of rocks!

NEIL: Look for a smooth place.

BUZZ (looking out the window): I don't see one, Neil.

NEIL: *Eagle* to Mission Control. Come in Mission Control.

MISSION CONTROL: Mission Control here.

NEIL: The Sea of Tranquility is covered with rocks. We cannot land there. Repeat, we cannot land there.

MISSION CONTROL: Continue to monitor the computer, *Eagle*.

NEIL: The computer's leading us into the rocks, Mission Control. Request permission to override and switch to manual control.

MISSION CONTROL: Stand by, *Eagle*. Continue to monitor computer.

BUZZ: We can't do that. Those rocks are getting too close.

NEIL: Cannot do that, Mission Control.

MISSION CONTROL: You do not have enough fuel for manual control, *Eagle*.

BUZZ: Neil, we're getting close. We don't have much time.

NEIL: *Eagle* is switching to manual control, Mission Control.

NARRATOR 2: Neil turns off the computer and takes the controls. An alarm immediately goes off.

BUZZ: Uh-oh, low fuel alert.

NEIL: How much do we have left?

BUZZ: About two minutes worth.

NEIL: Mission Control, *Eagle* is now searching for a landing site.

MISSION CONTROL: Fuel is low, *Eagle*.

NEIL: We're aware of that, Mission Control. (He looks out of the window.) I think I see a clear spot.

MISSION CONTROL: One minute of fuel left, *Eagle*.

NEIL: Almost there . . .

MISSION CONTROL: Forty-five seconds . . .

NEIL: We're over the spot. Fire the retro rockets.

BUZZ: Roger.

MISSION CONTROL: Forty seconds . . .

NEIL: We're going down.

MISSION CONTROL: *Eagle,* your landing spot may not be firm enough to hold the craft.

NEIL: We have no choice, Mission Control. We're going down.

BUZZ: Almost there, Neil.

MISSION CONTROL: Thirty seconds of fuel left . . .

NEIL: We're about to touch down.

NARRATOR 1: The *Eagle* lands with a small bump. There is no more movement.

MISSION CONTROL: *Eagle*—are you there?

NEIL: Tranquility Base here. The *Eagle* has landed.

MISSION CONTROL: Roger, *Eagle*. Nice job. You are now cleared to take a nap for the next four hours—

NEIL AND BUZZ: A nap?!

BUZZ: No way! We want to get out there!

NEIL: Mission Control, request permission to explore the surface of the moon.

MISSION CONTROL: You two should rest—

NEIL: We didn't fly to the moon to take a nap.

MISSION CONTROL: Permission granted, *Eagle.*

SCENE 2: Surface of the moon. Neil, now in his full space suit, steps down the ladder on the side of the *Eagle.*

NEIL: I've reached the bottom of the ladder . . . I'm standing on the pad . . . I'm now stepping off the pad . . . (*He steps on the surface of the moon.*) That's one small step for man, one giant leap for mankind.

MISSION CONTROL: How does it look, Commander?

NEIL: Dark . . . there are some rocks . . . lots of desolation.

MISSION CONTROL: Not much out there, huh, Commander?

NEIL: No, but it's beautiful.

NARRATOR 2: After a few minutes, Buzz joined Neil on the moon's surface. They took soil samples, performed scientific experiments, and planted an American flag. After about two-and-a-half hours, the two men went back into the *Eagle* and successfully flew back to the *Columbia.* All three astronauts returned safely to Earth on July 24, 1969. President Richard Nixon flew halfway around the world to greet them. A huge ticker-tape parade was held in their honor in New York City. The astronauts' next trips were tamer: They visited a total of 22 countries and were greeted by thousands of people. The next year Neil Armstrong retired from NASA. His footprints are still visible on the surface of the moon.

Neil Armstrong
Teaching Guide

Neil Armstrong was born on August 5, 1930, in Wapakoneta, Ohio. When he was two years old, his grandfather took him to an air show to see stunt fliers, and his love of aviation was born. As a boy, Armstrong designed and flew model airplanes. In 1947, he entered Purdue University to study engineering on a Navy scholarship. While he was at Purdue, the Korean War broke out, and the Navy called him up as a pilot. Neil Armstrong flew 78 combat missions in Korea. After the war, he went to Edwards Air Force Base as a civilian test pilot, where he set altitude records in such aircraft as the X-1 and X-15. Armstrong became an astronaut in 1962 and commanded the *Gemini 8* and *Apollo 11* missions, and was the first man to walk on the moon. He retired from astronaut duty in 1970 and returned to live in Ohio in 1971. He lives there today with his wife Janet and sons Ricky and Mark.

Book Links

Neil Armstrong: Space Pioneer by Paul Westman (Lerner, 1980)

Liftoff: The Story of America's Adventures in Space by Michael Collins (Gore, 1988)

To Space and Back by Sally Ride and Susan Okie (Lothrop, 1986)

EXTENSION ACTIVITIES

Talk About It

☆ **PASTIMES TO PAYCHECKS:** Although Neil Armstrong knew from an early age that he wanted to fly, he probably didn't imagine that he would fly to the moon one day. What kinds of activities do your students enjoy? In which activities do they feel they excel? List these activities on the chalkboard. Talk about why students enjoy doing these particular things. Challenge them to share how they might be able to channel these skills into careers when they are adults. Do the possibilities interest them?

☆ **LIST OF FIRSTS:** Neil Armstrong was the first person to set foot on the moon. Jackie Robinson was the first African American player to break into the all-white major leagues. Amelia Earhart was the first pilot to fly from California to Hawaii. In a brainstorming session, let students develop a list of "firsts" that remain to be accomplished. Which ones would they like to be the first person to achieve? Do they feel that there are no longer as many "firsts" to achieve today as there once were?

Write About It

⭐ **THE RIGHT STUFF:** The three astronauts on the *Apollo 11* mission had to face the possibility that they might not make it back to earth. When Neil Armstrong stepped onto the moon's surface, he was stepping into the unknown. Ask students to write about times when they've had to face the unknown. How did they feel before and after the experiences? What did they learn? Did they consider themselves courageous? What do students think would have happened if they had given in to their fears?

⭐ **ROLE PLAY:** As Neil Armstrong and Buzz Aldrin approached the moon, they saw that the original landing site was unsafe, but Mission Control told them to stay with the computer. When have students had to tell someone in authority that he or she was wrong? How did they present their points? Did they get in trouble, or were they proved right in the end? Have students recreate the situations by writing dialogues between themselves and the people whose authority they felt they had to override. You may wish to have students choose partners and then perform their dialogues for the rest of the class.

Be sure to give students opportunities to share their writing via read-alouds, bulletin boards, writing walls, learning centers, and so on.

Report About It

⭐ **SPACEY TIME LINE:** Since President Kennedy issued the call for space travel, many people have participated in making that a reality. Have students choose one decade—the 60s, 70s, 80s, or 90s—and select one person involved in the space program during that time period to research. When the reports are finished, ask students to use them to prepare a time line that charts the history of the space program.

⭐ **MARS, ANYONE?:** Do students think they have the right stuff to become astronauts? In this two-part activity, ask them to find out what kind of training people must go through before going into space. Then students should choose one of the planets or its satellites—or another point in space—to explore. They should explore the following questions in their reports: How long will their trip take? What should they expect to find when they land their spacecrafts? What will the atmosphere and the climate be like? How much will they weigh? How long will the days and nights be? What kinds of special precautions will they need to take?

NOTES

NOTES

NOTES

NOTES

NOTES